About the Author

Originally from Penang, Malaysia, Kwan Kew Lai attended Wellesley College on a full scholarship, paving the way for her to become a doctor. In 2005, she left her position as a professor of medicine to dedicate time to humanitarian work: in HIV/AIDS in Africa and to provide disaster relief all over the world, during wars, famine, and natural disasters, including the Ebola outbreak, the Syrian, Rohingya refugee crises, Yemen, and the COVID-19 pandemic in New York and the Navajo Nation. She is a three-time recipient of the President's Volunteer Service Award.

kwankewlai.com

Kwan Kew Lai

The Girl Who Taught Herself to Fly

www.vineleavespress.com

Print Edition
ISBN: 978-618-86002-8-7
Published by Vine Leaves Press in Greece 2022

Cover design by Jessica Bell
Interior design by Amie McCracken

A catalogue record of this work is available from The National Library of Greece.

*This book is dedicated to my mother
whose resilience and resourcefulness
saw us through innumerable difficult times,
to my father who I believe was proud of his children,
to Wellesley College for reaching
halfway around the world,
offering an impoverished young woman
the opportunity to fulfill her dreams,
and to all the girls and women
who are still fighting
for their rights to an education.*

Part I
To be born a girl

1

Oh, to be able to fly

My life changed when Ah Yee, my mother, enrolled me in primary school. I was a fledgling, slowly growing her feathers and preparing her wings for a long flight into self-determination and independence.

Before then I watched with envy as droves of Tamil girls went to the school across from my home, to learn to read and write. They wore clean blue and white uniforms, carrying their school books in their shoulder bags, while I was the street urchin who remained uneducated, whiling away my time conceiving ways to play pranks on them.

On our way home from Kong Ming Chinese Primary School, my second sister, Kuan May, who was two years older than me, occasionally took a shortcut through the Tamil Indian village. The Tamils lived in mud-houses next to a few open stalls where they kept their cattle and goats. The ground was always wet with cow dung and urine, and on rainy days, rivulets of animal waste filled the paths; we picked our way with great care around the puddles, trying to keep our white shoes white. The overwhelming stench defeated our effort of covering our noses with our handkerchiefs.

The Indians' houses were made of mud mixed with straw and cow dung. The women drew *kolam* early in the morning. After sweeping a patch of dirt at the front door of their homes and dousing it with water, they sprinkled finely ground rice flour freehand and with little hesitation created symmetric and geometric designs of vines and flowers. The *kolam* was a sign of invitation to welcome all into their home, including Lakshmi, the goddess of prosperity and wealth, and it prevented evil spirits from entering.

A little Indian girl cared for her baby brothers, playing on a small patch of concrete floor at the back of their house, surrounded by dirt, dung, and mud. The Indian girl's dress, brown with dirt, was missing a shoulder strap. It draped across her chest, barely covering her nipple. No sunlight penetrated the thick waxy foliage of a mango tree; her corner of the world was dark and dingy. She flashed a shy smile when we ran by. A woman, hair done up in a bun, hunched over a stove with blinding and choking fumes rising from the fire she had started with dried cowdung and coconut husks, yelled at the girl to fetch a pot from the house. Hidden in a forsaken corner of the earth, the government was not likely to discover a lone girl whose parents broke the law for not sending their children to the mandatory primary school.

One day when we took this shortcut, Kuan May and I stopped in our tracks. The Indian girl was dressed in bright silk while her brothers remained in tatters. Her face was powdered white, her eyes were outlined in black kohl, and her fingers were stained with henna. A colorful and glittery scarf draped over her head and numerous gold bangles dangled from her wrists. Her feet remained bare except for encircling golden anklets and toe-rings, and her nails were painted bright red. Her resplendence contrasted with the dark, squalid ambiance of the back of the mud house. Despite the stench we stood transfixed, admiring her transformed appearance, unsure why she was so richly attired. The red *bindi* on her forehead gave her away. At thirteen, although she looked more like ten, she had become a married woman.

By a cement tank outside the house, a grown Indian man splashed and poured a bucket of water over his curly black hair, taking his bucket bath. He had hair growing from his chest all the way down below his navel. Apart from a dirty loincloth, he was naked. We averted our eyes and ran past him.

Was this grown man, twice her size, her husband? He could have been her father. Did he live in the same village and own many head of cattle? A good marriage for her according to the Indian tradition.

Soon the little Indian girl's belly began to swell. Less than a year after she was married, she cradled her baby while still caring for her younger brothers. All while Kuan May and I continued running back and forth from school to home. Her world remained the same patch of concrete floor surrounded by the cow stalls and stench, her baby in a pack on her back while she prepared the family meals.

A frightening thought crossed my mind: What if my father decided to marry us off the same way? I shuddered.

Ah Yee, my mother, certainly could not prevent this from happening. She could not stop him from giving her baby, Wan, away to his brother, even before the baby was weaned. She was not even included in the discussion and had no say whatsoever.

I wanted to see the world and not be bound to a small forgotten fragment of the earth. I wanted to be free from the island's traditional marriage role for women.

I thought hard for days for a solution and concluded that if this was going to happen to me, I would run away. But where and how? Looming, troubling questions requiring urgent answers.

And I had none.

From that day on, I worked doubly hard at school. Somehow my racked brain told me that to get out of a world where girls had almost no control of their future, I had to excel in my education; I had to dig myself out.

Many women of my mother's generation married through arranged marriages. The parents of my peers, especially those from the low-income group, took them out of school to help raise younger siblings and earn money, eventually marrying them off.

Like Ah Yee, they were soon burdened with children. They lived with their parents-in-law and helped with chores, under the stern rule of their mothers-in-law. We counted ourselves lucky my father had not forced us to drop out of school to help him full time in his food stall. If he ever did, I hoped Ah Wee, my adopted brother, would intervene. By that time, he was working full-time and helping with the family expenses; he carried a certain amount of financial clout to sway my father's decision.

My mother was a very fertile woman; she was in a perpetual state of pregnancy, breastfeeding, or cradling a baby. No sooner had a baby been weaned from her breasts then she was pregnant again; sometimes she became pregnant even before the baby was weaned. She never had time to recover from her previous pregnancy and remained thin, always nurturing life in or out of her womb, having hardly any surplus to fuel her fat reserves. She had so many children to take care of, a whole house to clean, laundry to be washed by hand and ironed with an old coal-fueled iron, and meals to prepare. Our stove was stoked either with coals or firewood which she chopped, and she had to boil water for drinking; laborious physical work that had to be done with a lot of planning. There was hardly any time left for herself. She warmed the water to bathe the children since she believed cold water caused sickness or could scare the soul out of a baby. One might as well be as good as dead with a soulless body.

Ah Yee made diapers from linen or cotton *sarong* she bought in the market, cutting the material into squares and folding the squares into triangles. When she had no spare cash to buy new linen, she tore up her old *sarong*. She soaked the soiled ones overnight in a bucket of detergent. In the morning she hand-washed them and hung them on the lines to dry. Her hands became red, raw, and rough from all the hard work.

With the first batch of babies, my father arranged for help around the house for a month so she could devote her attention to the baby and recover from childbirth. As time went on, he stopped getting her the extra help. We pitched in and helped with the household chores. She ate special rice fried in sesame oil and ginger and drank the red post-partum wine, but they no longer lasted for an entire month.

One evening, as was typical, my father sat at the dinner table chewing his food, savoring the Tiger beer from a big mug, foam forming a mustache on his upper lip. Tapping his chopsticks impatiently on the side of a bowl, he grumbled as the specters of his discontent happened to pass through the kitchen.

"*Gao liau bu-iong.*" Useless lots. Although my father was Hakka, he spoke to us in the Hokkien dialect of Penang Island, the Chinese dialect of most of the islanders, the so-called *Nanyan* or the South Seas Chinese. The Hakka Chinese are largely descended from North Han Chinese in the northern provinces of China and migrated and settled in Southern China. In the nineteenth century, many Hakka and *Nanyan* Chinese, including my father's parents, migrated to Malaya. Ah Yee was Teochew but she spoke Hakka and Hokkien.

My father considered us girls Ah Yee's children, and he had nothing to do with us. Whenever we did anything wrong, he said to her, "*Lu eh cha-bó-kiá.*" These are your daughters.

It had been several years since my mother first gave birth to a baby boy, a *ta-po-kiá,* my brother Boon. He desperately wanted another.

Throwing down his chopsticks on the table, he pushed his chair back and got up with a loud groan. He had lost his appetite after such an unappetizing monologue. Ah Yee seldom if ever offered her opinion. He said, "*Chooi kam kim,*" literally holding gold in one's mouth, afraid to lose it if one opens one's mouth to speak, referring to Ah Yee's silence. Wobbling to the front porch, he took out his folding reclining chair, slowly lowered himself into it, lit his pipe, and began puffing. The drink took effect and soon he began to snore.

While Ah Yee never argued with him when he blamed her for birthing the girls, my oldest sister Fong, his first-born, was not so reticent. Her nursing school education taught her the sex of a baby was a contribution from both parents. Their argument often got heated, but through it all, Ah Yee remained taciturn.

Finally, the heavens must have heard my father's prayer for whenever he could he went to the temples to burn joss sticks and incense, praying to the gods to bless him with another boy. Ah Yee's eighth baby was a *ta-po-kiá*, my brother Beng, born when I was eight years old. Happy at last, he celebrated the occasion with a bottle of Guinness Stout while it was Ah Wee who bought a bottle of post-partum red wine for Ah Yee. Father bragged about his *ta-po-kiá* to all his friends.

As a baby, Beng was prone to asthmatic attacks and frightened us when he experienced difficulty breathing. Such attacks always happened in the middle of the night. Ah Yee held his limp body, screaming. One night his asthma was so bad all we could hear was the loud wheezing, he looked exhausted and blue. Kuan May and I ran to the sundry store to wake up the shopkeeper, he owned a Ford. Ah Wee carried Beng to the car and they drove to the hospital. He ended up hospitalized for over a week and did not outgrow his asthma until he was much older.

When Ah Yee became pregnant for the ninth time, she consulted our neighbor Fat Choo who loaned her money during hard times, wanting to know how to get rid of it.

Snapping green beans at the kitchen table, she said to Ah Yee, "*Jiak ong lai,*" Eat pineapples. Apparently, she believed that eating anything sour would cause the womb to contract and push the baby out.

In the fruit orchard, a few anemic pineapple bushes grew under the dense shade of the rambutan trees, but they failed to produce any fruits. Ah Yee had to spend what little she had to buy them from the market.

One day, waves of abdominal cramps overcame her. She lay on the floor next to my father's cot, groaning. Thick dark slimy fluid oozed between her legs and through her *sarong*. She asked Kuan May to hurry and fetch Fat Choo.

Fat Choo came running in her wooden clogs, her bosom heaved and bounced below her *sarong*, "*Aiyo, lueh bui see?*" You want to die?

She washed Ah Yee and tucked her in bed while I prayed to God to spare her life. Ah Yee rested in bed for a few days, then got up and wobbled to the kitchen to resume being our mother again. She had lost that baby, but a few months passed and her belly grew big again. Alas, it was another *cha-bó-kiá*, a girl!

Upset, my father stayed away from home till late, returning drunk. Skipping dinner, he changed into his *sarong,* went straight to bed, and never once took a look at the baby.

Ah Yee did not try to get rid of her subsequent pregnancies after the scary attempt.

Perpetually short of food, we were often hungry even though my father's share of dinner was always plentiful. Each night one of us placed a stake for his left-overs which invariably there would be, for he was a small eater. What with snacks at the *toddy* shop or *kopitiam*, coffee shop, and more drinking at home, his belly became full quickly. Just as soon as he left the dinner table, we all partook of the left-over food like vultures.

"*Iao lau kao.*" Hungry monkeys, Ah Yee called us as she eyed the dishes with longing but she never touched a morsel. When Ah Wee worked late, she set aside a generous portion of the dinner for him. He often ate at work and because he had a delicate stomach, eating before bedtime caused him heartburn. Ah Yee left the best part of the meals for her children and her husband, eating the least desirable parts of a chicken such as the head, neck, feet, and the bishop's nose, the head of a fish or the fatty part of pork when we had meat in our diet, which was rare. She became increasingly thin and malnourished.

In the Malay house, my parents slept in the same room with us. I slept on the floor directly next to their bed. Their rhythmic lovemaking often woke me up, watching the wrought iron bed and its canopy rocking synchronously with their bodies. Many nights I lay awake waiting for my father to get up from the cot, hitching his *sarong* as he picked his way over our sleeping bodies to go to Ah Yee.

Even in my young mind, I knew that was how my parents made their babies. Later in our home at Hye Keat Estate, my parents had their own bedroom, the wrought iron bed took up most of the floor. It fitted snugly with its three sides against the walls, leaving space on the fourth wall for Ah Yee's wardrobe. My parents continued to sleep with the youngest baby. I did not have to witness them making love anymore. But since Ah Yee continued to be pregnant, it was certainly still happening.

At eighteen, Fong had had enough. She asked my father to curb his sexual appetite and reminded him of his parental responsibilities of child-rearing. He was well into his sixties by then. Fong asked Ah Yee to stop having babies. Ah Yee gave her a blank stare. All her life she could never say no to my father when he came to her at night.

In nursing school, Fong had learned about the birth-control pill. The good news was Ah Yee could get it free from the local government clinic. The pill, she told her, would stop her from making any more babies, and she need not have to tell my father about it. Fong accompanied her to the local clinic, but she became pregnant again, much to my brother Boon's consternation. Boon was her first son who was also training to be a hospital assistant in the same nursing school as Fong.

He asked her, "*In hô tōa-pak-tó?*" Why does your belly continue to get big? Ah Yee admitted she had forgotten to take the pills. The family planning nurse came for a home visit, fortunately, my father was not home.

When she reached term with her twelfth and last baby, she experienced contractions during the day but continued her chores until evening. Only then did she pack a small bag and Kuan May and I walked her to the bus station, a mile away. She boarded the bus; there was no money for bus fare for us. I felt a deep sadness watching her climb up the stairs into the bus alone. Where it dropped her off, she had to walk another mile to reach the maternity hospital, all in the midst of her labor pangs.

In the evening my father came home and learned that Ah Yee was in the maternity hospital. He ate his dinner by himself and drank his Tiger beer, we all stayed away from him. The next day he biked to the hospital to visit her. To his great disappointment, she had another *cha-bó-kiá*. When he returned at the end of the day, the glum, drawn look on his face told us all too well he had not gotten his boy.

Ah Yee came home with Ean. She walked with her legs spread apart in obvious discomfort, having to deal with fresh wounds from the delivery, never once complaining about my father or getting mad at him.

Ean means swallow in Chinese. Ah Yee's last baby became her favorite. My father wanted to give her away, but the older siblings intervened. My mother used her savings accumulated through the years from her other working children's financial contributions to put Ean through university. She became the first child to receive a university degree in Malaysia.

With the birth control pills, Ah Yee was free at last from the burden of perpetual pregnancy. My father never suspected his daughter and son had sabotaged him. He had attempted birth control before—I had found a condom in the fruit orchard many years before. Boon was already in nursing school and said it prevented babies from being made.

In my early teens, I made up my mind not to submit myself to living a life like Ah Yee, completely financially dependent on my father. Although given the choice and the right circumstances, she would have loved to find herself a job and be rid of her dependency. Her lack of education hampered her, and she was overburdened with too many children. She tried hard to be financially independent by raising her brood of fowls, but that was fraught with uncertainty. I remembered the little Indian girl living on a small forgotten patch of the earth. The solution for me to escape the cycle of poverty was to get a good education, a career, and not be financially dependent on a man. Even if I did get married I would have a say in what I could and could not do.

When I was six, living in the orchard with the wild fields at the back of our house, I watched the swallows, or the *burung layang-layang,* flying excitedly in the evening, swooping fast and low with their tuxedo scissor-like tails temptingly close to me, teasing and challenging me to follow their lead. It was then Ah Yee asked us what we imagined ourselves to be if we could change into an animal. I told her without hesitation I wished I could fly as free as a swallow. This thought stayed with me, and it spurred me to pursue a drastic course to leave my loved ones, my home, and my country to fulfill my dreams. I fell in love with the idea of being free, independent, and the one to steer my own destiny. I wanted to be like the swallow, the *burung layang-layang*, I wanted to be able to fly.

I never asked Ah Yee what she wished to be. Did she also dream about being free to choose, and oh, to be able to fly?

2
"I have eaten more salt than you have eaten rice."

My father had twelve children: two boys and ten girls, and according to him, a family big enough to form a football team. Before his biological children came to the scene, he had the custody of three children: a boy and two girls. He was proud of the size of his family; perhaps it showed the world his prowess and fecundity as a man since he was still having children when he was well into his sixties. He had proved his manhood. Nevertheless, the idea of a football team consisting of crawling babies, toddlers, teenagers, girls, and boys seemed absurd and often troubled me. We would surely lose.

The boys were special in his eyes and as far as he was concerned, they could do no wrong. Fate was destined to spite him. His firstborn was a girl, my sister Fong, who had a temper equal to his. By all accounts, he doted on her and admired her courage to argue with him and to stand her ground for what she thought was right. Fong was born close to the end of the Second World War when everything was scarce. Lack of food and stress caused my young mother to be unable to make enough milk to satisfy the baby's hunger. My father had to bike for miles to buy milk powder and condensed milk in the black market.

In my mind, I conjured up images of him biking through Japanese sentries and barbwire and paying some shady men an exorbitant fee for the milk. We all knew about him traveling long distances, braving danger for Fong, because he took every opportunity to remind her of this whenever she angered him with her impudent remarks and rebellious behavior. He wanted to hammer that fact into her head, so she would be forever grateful to him. But that usually produced the opposite result.

He was rewarded with an heir when his second-born, my brother Boon, arrived. A cause for celebration, he announced the birth to the neighbors, giving away baskets of hard-boiled eggs dyed red, symbolizing good luck and prosperity. My mother was mollycoddled for a month when my father hired an *amah* to care for her and the baby, and to do the household chores.

At the end of the month, my brother's head was shaved, and the neighbors were invited to a banquet to celebrate his survival past the most dangerous part of an infant's life. Unfortunately, it also signaled the end of my mother's brief pampered existence.

There was not much fanfare when the third child, Kuan May, and the fourth—me—arrived. We were mere girls, hardly reason enough for my father to open his wallet and splurge to announce to the world of our arrival. We would not be able to carry on the family name and we were a constant reminder of his failure to produce another male child.

After three more girls, my mother gave birth to a spare, her eighth child, my frail younger brother Beng. My brother's name means brightness, as though my father was thankful to be given a bright ray of hope after so many years of darkness, despair, and deep disappointment.

Fong was feisty, outspoken, unafraid of him, and constantly argued with him. Despite the incessant bickering, my father had a lot of respect for her. For her alone, he changed his standard view on girls.

Stripped down to his boxer's shorts, my father turned around in his chair and looked at us sternly over the rims of his spectacles. We were then scattered on the floor doing our homework, since there was only a single table to accommodate a few of us and my father was taking up one of the few spaces.

"If I die, Fong will be in charge of you all," he said, meaning she would be responsible for bringing all of us up and providing for us. That was not what she wanted to hear.

With her sharp tongue, she wasted no time reminding him, "I did not ask to be born, and I did not bring your children into this world. You are responsible for them even if you are dead."

A shudder of fear trickled down my spine, waiting for his thunderous reaction.

There was none, just ponderous silence.

I once had the courage to ask him why girls were so dispensable to him, why we were useless.

He stared at me with a look that implied I had asked a stupid question not deserving of an answer. A disquiet hung in the air as he turned his attention to what he was doing, playing solitaire with a stern concentrated expression of knitted eyebrows, taking meditative and deliberate puffs on his pipe.

His bent head, with the pink scalp peeping through his thinning crown of salt and pepper hair, nodded rhythmically with the shaking of his legs, he grunted and snorted a reply, *"Wah jiak kiam tua lu jiak png!"* quoting a Chinese saying which literally means I have eaten more salt than you have eaten rice!

I pictured the enormous pile of salt that he had eaten in his life to that of my small pile of rice in my short life; was he trying to tell me I would never be able to amass the great wealth of his life experience and achieve the height of his wisdom no matter how long I lived.

Once we girls were married, our children would take on the surname of our husbands, virtually ending his family line. To him, this was tantamount to feeding us with what he called *see png* or *dead rice*—money he spent on food that would not benefit him in the long run but only the family into which we would be married—a tremendous waste.

A fervent believer in ancestral worship, the restless spirits of his dead and starving ancestors would roam the world if the living children did not provide them with food offerings.

Unlike his daughters, his sons would carry on the family name and would be sure to provide for them—and him—in the afterworld.

Sending his daughters to school was akin to spending money for the families into which they would be married. It made no sense to him to continue our education. Fortunately for us, he would break the law if he did not send us to primary school. After his mandatory retirement from government service at age fifty-five, he worked long hours seven days a week hawking food on a bicycle cart and later, running a food stall. Earning a living consumed all of his time, forcing him to rise early in the morning and return late in the evening; he was too tired to care if we were still in school. He never quite remembered when we finished primary school and was oblivious when we continued with our secondary school education. We received no interference from him.

In the Chinese culture, even rearing a cockerel or a dog is more useful than raising a girl as a local Hokkien ditty *Eh Lo Kay* seems to imply.

Eh lo kay, chai bee chai chek, lai chee kay,
Chee kay, gau kiow kare,
Chee kow, gau booi mei,
Chee thow sneh, yang lau peh,
Chee chow war, hor lang meh.

Eh lo kay, plant rice, plant paddy, to feed the chickens,
Rear a cockerel, it crows at dawn,
Rear a dog, it barks at night,
Raise a son, he will carry his father,
Raise a daughter and you will be scorned.

Eh lo kay,
Tho bee tho chek, lai chee kay,
Chee chow war, par lang ay,
Chee thow sneh, kor lau peh.

Eh loy kay,
Beg for rice, beg for paddy, to feed the chickens,
Raise a daughter, she belongs to another,
Raise a son, he will take care of his father.

I grew up hearing the constant banter and the reminders of the uselessness of the female persuasion; I vowed secretly I would prove my father wrong. I knew enough not to open my mouth for fear of inciting his unpredictable and fiery temper and testing his hand with the feather duster cane on me.

To Malaysians in those days, Australia was like the United States to many potential immigrants: a land of opportunities. It was fashionable for well-to-do families to send their children to Australia for higher education if England was beyond their reach. Many young Malaysians settled there after attending universities and did not return to their homeland—a brain drain for the young country.

For some strange reason, my father had the idea he would one day send me to Australia and he boasted to his friends who would listen, telling them I was the smart one. I was flattered and secretly hoped this miracle would happen, but I knew full well he had no financial means to do so. It was just a pipe dream.

By then it was clear I was doing very well in school, much more brilliantly than his first male child, Boon, who almost did not go on to secondary school because he scored too low for his entrance examination. My father was so concerned for him, he made time to go to the school, along with many other worried parents, waiting to see what would be decided for their sons. That year fortune smiled on Boon as the education department lowered the entrance requirement.

If I was going to prove my father wrong about his long-held belief of the uselessness of girls in this world, I would have to perform a miracle of my own.

3

The fourth child

"Ah Yee, Ah Yee, *manna* Ah Keow?" Ahmadkan, my Malay playmate pounded on the backdoor, asking my mother where I was. Ah Yee means auntie in Hokkien.

I was born at sunrise in 1950, in the year of the Tiger of the Chinese lunar calendar, in Georgetown, Penang, a tropical island in the Andaman Sea, off the west coast of the Malay Peninsula. Ah Yee said I was a morning tiger and according to her I was a good tiger because I had hunted, was satiated, and would not be of harm to anyone. The British, who named the town after their monarch King George the Third, also named Penang Island after the Prince of Wales. It was also known as the Pearl of the Orient or Pulau Mutiara, but the locals kept its original name, Pulau Pinang—the Island of the Areca Nut Palms.

When Sir Francis Light landed on the island, there was an abundance of areca nut palms. It was ceded to the English East India Company on August 11, 1786, by Sultan Abdullah Mukarram, the ruler of Kedah in exchange for British protection from Siamese and Burmese threats. In

29

1826, Penang became the first Straits Settlement of the British crown colony, followed by Singapore and Malacca in the Strait of Malacca.

My parents were married during the Second World War, in June 1944 and were busy making babies soon after. Fong, the eldest, was born five months before the end of the war and Boon, a year and a half later. They should have stopped then; they would have had a perfect family of four.

My parents had more children than Penang had names. Within the span of nine years, five children were born. I was the fourth child and by the time the fifth baby, my sister, Lian Hua, came along, my mother had her hands full and was too busy to take care of me. She sent me to Ahmadkan's family, our Malay Muslim neighbors. Every morning, he came running to the back of the house, peering through the screen door of the kitchen calling for me. I was four years old and did not feel abandoned, or that my mother loved me less. I was just game for adventures outside my home.

I do not know how my parents picked our names. I doubt Ah Yee was ever involved. She had started school at a late age and had only a week of class before the Japanese invasion closed all schools. My father's friend, Mr. Li, a trustee of Kong Ming Chinese Primary School, spoke fluent Mandarin. Perhaps my father consulted him.

Once my father chose our names, he had to register at the birth registry to get our birth certificates. The anglophone bureaucrat who transcribed the phoneme spelled our surname in two different ways, Lai and Lye, so on paper some of us were not related to each other. He consulted the book of names for the Lai family and all his children were to have the same generation name of the phoneme of Kuan like

Kuan Yin, the Goddess of Mercy. The registrar completely mutilated it and it appeared in a variety of ways for the twelve children: Khoon, Kon, Kow, Kuan, and Kwan. Our third name was our given name, a unique name for each of us. My given name Kew, pronounced Keow in our dialect of Hakka, was spelled Kew by the registrar, the same way it would be pronounced by the Cantonese. Most of my father's generation was uneducated and, having an authoritative official barking or pronouncing a name that sounded close to the name he envisioned it to be, he was likely to nod his head in agreement.

When I was born, we were still under British colonial rule. Did the registrar, if he were an Englishman, spell my name after the Kew Gardens in England? Kew in Mandarin indicates feminine beauty or coquettishness. Together with my middle name, Kwan, which means to look, celebrate, or appreciate, had Mr. Li discerned a degree of femininity in the baby when he first set eyes on me?

We lived on River Road close to Sungai Pinang or the Penang River in the first house of a row of four terraced stucco government houses with asbestos roofing. My father worked for the government as a switchgear inspector in charge of a crew of linesmen of Tamil Indians, descendants of laborers from south India, transplanted by the British East India Company during the eighteenth and nineteenth centuries. At that rank, the government gave him the use of one of these comfortable two-bedroom houses. As ours was at the end of a row, we were fortunate to have windows welcoming in the daylight.

Ahmadkan's house sat alone on an expansive field to the right of my house, atop concrete stilts four feet above the ground like most Malay houses. Instead of an *attap* or thatched roof, it had a corrugated asbestos roof. His father was a caretaker for the local mosque.

The island swarmed with children—the result of the baby boom after the Second World War. To accommodate them, the schools were divided into morning and afternoon sessions. Fong had morning school. My father took her to the Convent Chinese Primary Girls' School on his bicycle on his way to work. Boon had school in the afternoon, and he was already busy exploring the muddy river with the boys in the neighborhood by the time I got up. Being a boy, he was free to roam on his own, indulging in his exploits. Kuan May devoted her time to playing with Meng Ling, our neighbors' daughter, who was close to her age.

I have no memory of what I looked like. My mother never took me to the photo studio. The other children all had their baby pictures taken either alone or with my mother, including the fifth baby, Lian Hua. She had skipped me, the fourth child—no baby pictures taken for posterity.

Thye, my adopted sister, and my mother had a picture together with their hair in victory rolls. Kuan May had a picture of herself crawling on a carpeted floor, dolled up in a frilly dress and ruffled socks. There was a picture of my mother sitting on a chair holding Kuan May, with Fong standing, together with her best friend, Chooi Ee, and her only daughter, Ah Chui, wearing floral *sam foo* looking intently at the camera. There were photographs of my parents and their friends posing on their veranda and going on outings with Boon, who recalled squashing and beating down Ah Yee's puffed-up *sarong*, while she was in a pool. I was twelve when I had my very first photograph taken for a government-issued identification card. I had on my primary school blouse, the best clothes I owned.

I was born left-handed. It was bad luck to be a leftie since the left hand was considered unclean, it was delegated to cleaning one's private parts while the right hand was reserved for eating and writing. My mother tried to cure me of my left-handedness by hitting my left hand when I grabbed a spoon with it to eat. Being the fourth child might have had something to do with my having no baby pictures taken at all. Four is an unlucky number. The phoneme for the number four in Hokkien is nearly homophonous with the word death. Perhaps the fourth child would bring bad luck when she appeared in the photograph with the family, she might even invite death into their midst!

My mother rose early to get breakfast ready and took great pains to get me dressed, since I had to appear well-groomed for Ahmadkan's mother. My adopted sisters took care of my baby sister Lian Hua. With all her children taken care of, she went to the wet market to buy food for the family. There was no refrigeration—food was purchased, cooked, and consumed for the day.

Ahmadkan was a thin, agile Malay Muslim boy with skin as tanned as his tousled nut-brown hair, in contrast to my fair complexion and neatly combed wavy black hair. We ran through the wet dewy green field, disturbing the delicate pink, feathery mimosa flowers or touch-me-not. The mimosa leaves promptly closed as our legs brushed against them. The searing heat of the full sun evaporated the moisture, and the humidity hung heavy, even early in the morning. We ran underneath his house, scattering the frightened chickens, and raced up the back stairs. A hen cackled and looked at us with a disapproving gaze, coaxing her chicks to come under her wings to safety while the indignant rooster strutted about, head held high, straightening his neck and opening his beak to let out a long, loud warning crow.

A delicious breakfast awaited us in the kitchen, *nasi lemak*—rice steamed in coconut milk, *ikan bilis* or dried anchovies, and groundnuts wrapped in banana leaf. Ahmadkan's mother added a generous scoop of spicy *sambal* for herself but was more circumspect with my portion. Sitting right on top of all this was one half of a hard-boiled egg and a slice or two of cooling cucumber, offering some solace to the tongue for the hot *sambal*.

Boon nicknamed me "fatty" because I was chubby with rolls of baby fat. My mother blamed Ahmadkan's mother for my plumpness, feeding me all that rich Malay food.

His father came back for lunch on his bicycle and changed from his white shirt, white *sarong,* and black *songkok*— his Malay hat—into his blue and white checked *sarong*. He remained shirtless; it seemed pointless to wear a shirt when it would invariably be drenched from sweat while eating the mid-day meal.

His mother passed along a bar of soap, a pitcher of water, and a basin for us to wash our hands. We sat cross-legged on mats eating lunch with our fingers, pickled vegetables, *kankong belachan*, water convolvulus stir-fried with prawn paste, or chicken *rendang*. On other days the fare might be beef *rendang*, fried squid, cuttlefish, cockles, or *kerang*. The British, despite their almost two hundred years of presence in Penang, did not make a mark on the local cuisine other than introducing afternoon tea.

During the month of Ramadan, a lone Muslim man dressed in a black cloak walked through the village swinging a kerosene lamp, waking the Malays before dawn to eat *sahur*, the pre-dawn meal. The light from his lamp lit his face and threw a circle of dim halo around him—a ghost-like floating specter drifting down the row of terraced houses. The Muslims had to stop eating and drinking when the call for prayer came piping out from the mosque. He reappeared after sundown to signal time for the breaking of the fast, as though they needed reminding. I never envied the Malay children for having to get up so early to have their breakfast.

Ramadan was a trying time for my mother and me. There were no visits to Ahmadkan's house, and I stayed home. It usually fell in the rainy season in Penang. In the morning, I could only sit in the kitchen over a bowl of egg-drop soup, looking mournfully across the field. Relentless sheets of torrential rain obscured his house while I dreamed of having my breakfast there.

4

My mother, the third wife and her Cinderella story

My mother was seventeen when she married my father, who was forty-two. She was an orphan raised by her aunt and grandmother. She was never quite sure whether her aunt was her true blood relation. Back in Malaya, children often address older men and women as uncles and aunts as a polite way of greeting them, even if they are not relations.

My mother's name was Meng Kim or bright gold, but her skin was dark. Her marriage certificate stated that she hailed from the Teochew Province, Tar Por District in southern China. As long as her grandmother was alive she was protected from her aunt, who would have loved to make her do all the household chores and cater to her aunt's every need. Sticking close to her grandmother, she acquired all her culinary skills, mainly of the *nyonya* dishes. For several hundred years, intermarriages between the Straits Chinese immigrants and the Malays brought about a delicate culture of the *nyonyas* (the ladies) and the *babas* (the gentlemen). The resulting mixed heritage *Peranakans* were of darker skin color than the Chinese but lighter than that of the Malays. We could only speculate on her true heritage.

By the 1930s, numerous steamship lines connected Penang to the rest of the world, and it became an entertainment center with cabarets, cinemas, amusement parks, and gambling establishments. Born a few years before the crash of the stock market, Meng Kim started school quite late in her teenage years and recalled with fondness her one week of schooling before her education was prematurely ended by the Japanese invasion of Malaya on December 8, 1941, just an hour after the attack on Pearl Harbor. Penang was bombed, and the whole Malayan peninsula was quickly conquered by the devastating advance of the green-uniformed Japanese soldiers carrying weapons and grenades on their swift bicycles. The Bicycle Blitzkrieg, chased the British and their allies all the way to Singapore. From there the mighty British Royal Navy pulled out of the port heading to Australia, leaving the locals to the mercy of the troops of the Japanese Imperial Army. Meng Kim's life rapidly changed when the Empire of Japan took over British Malaya; the Japanese occupied the island, and the only relative she knew, her grandmother, passed away.

Like Cinderella, my mother became the maid of the house, at the beck and call of her aunt and her two daughters. With the Japanese occupation, her aunt sent her to work in one of the entertainment centers frequented by Japanese officers and soldiers. One night in the smoke-filled bar, a drunken officer stood at the bottom of the stairs ready to catch the first woman who came down. There was widespread panic and pandemonium while every woman tried to back as far away from the stairs as possible, screaming in terror. She never told us how it ended.

When she turned seventeen, a *mooi lang po*, a matchmaker, came to pay her aunt a visit. She claimed that my mother, who was born in the year of the rabbit of the Chinese lunar calendar, was well suited to be the wife of the man she had in mind for her. He was born in the year of the tiger, never mind that he already had three young children and needed a wife to take care of them. My father's ancestors were northern Chinese who had migrated to South China in the provinces of Guangdong, Fujian, Jiangxi, and Guangxi during the fall of the Nan Song dynasty in the 1270s. My grandfather came from the Fujian Province, Yong Ting District, and migrated to Singapore where my father was born at Bukit Timah. He was a Hakka, the Chinese characters for Hakka literally mean guest families, an outsider, an immigrant.

Later, after her marriage to my father, my mother learned that he had been married twice before and both his wives had died young. That seemed to be a bad omen, but her aunt could not care less. Details of the arranged marriage were not discussed with her and it was never an option for her to refuse. Where else would she go if she rejected this offer of marriage? She was sure her aunt would throw her out into the streets.

The day arrived when my father came along with the matchmaker to pick an auspicious date for the big day. My mother stole furtive glances from behind a curtain, her suitor was an *ah pawman*, a middle-aged man, hardly prince charming. Life with her aunt was never easy, at least with this man, she could start a new life. My father's name was Cheng Tong—the East was pure and bright.

Taken in June 1944, her wedding picture showed a tall, slender, demure woman standing half a foot apart from a man who was already showing some thinning of his hair and frontal balding with a broad forehead and bushy eyebrows; eyebrows that almost met in the middle above the bridge of his nose, very much like those of the Premier of China, Chou En-Lai. As my mother was taller than him, her gown draped around a stool on which he stood to render him additional inches. She never failed to mention this fact to us as she gazed at her faded, mottled wedding picture, she wearing a simple white, rented but elegant satin wedding gown, with a long organza veil trailing behind her, and in her hands, she held a bouquet of white lilies. Her veil rested softly over her slender shoulders upon which would soon be placed a heavy burden.

When my mother became my father's third wife, she instantly became a mother to two girls and a boy; his adopted children. Thye was seven years old, the apple of his eye. Rumors had it that she was his first wife's daughter, elevating her status in the household. Perhaps because of this, my mother was particularly strict with her and did not refrain from beating her for any small mistakes she made. When my father came home in the evenings, Thye would run to him for comfort and protection.

Next was Ah Wee, a dark five-year-old boy who had difficulty keeping his attendance in school. Truancy became the norm, and he soon dropped out. Always hungry, my mother would whack him on the head while he helped himself to a plate of food, taunting him for eating at her home without making any contribution. Boon was her precious little boy, unlike Ah Wee who was just an adopted kid. Her ill-treatment of Ah Wee so distressed Boon that he screamed at her and called her *ah bo tok*, the cruel woman, a derogatory name given to a stepmother. My father sent Ah Wee to work in a nearby abattoir, slaughtering chickens. With each paycheck, he dutifully handed most of his earnings to my mother, his contribution for his upkeep. She then complained less, grudgingly allowing him to eat his meager share of the food.

At low tide, the river that flowed alongside the abattoir was stained deep red and choked with feathers. Standing on the bridge over the river, I pictured Ah Wee killing chickens all day long. It never ceased to give me a deep sense of the horror of the inevitability of ending the life of a living creature. I was sorry he had to experience so much sorrow and death at such a young age.

Meng Kee was the youngest of the adopted children; a brooding, dark, mouth-pouting, quiet four-year-old girl, quick-tempered when provoked, with a skin color many shades darker than ours and eyes of deep pools. Her birth certificate registered her as a child born from a mother who was raped. She knew my mother was not her mother. She insisted she was born from a rock, relating it with such an intense look as though she wished to believe it was true that somewhere, somehow, she had a mother to call her own, even if it was a rock.

My father had a fourth child, Ah Sook, whom we never met. He was older than the rest of the adopted children who described him as short and stout and with unkempt, long, black hair. The several sketchbooks he left behind, stashed in my father's old cupboard, showed that he was a talented artist, sketching architectural buildings in precise and accurate perspective with detailed Corinthian and Ionian columns, but more gruesomely, severed heads presented on plates, eyes closed and hair tied up or draped over the faces, with blood trickling down the necks. Had the Japanese tortured and killed these people he depicted? Had he witnessed any of these grotesque scenes?

During the Japanese occupation, the Chinese were singled out as supporters of China where Japan had been waging the Second Sino-Japanese War since 1937. Thousands were rounded up and they disappeared during the Japanese reign of terror.

After the Second World War, the British returned to Malaya. A guerrilla war, the Malayan Emergency, and a communist insurgency started in 1948 and continued until 1960 joined by many locals who felt the British had let them down during the Second World War. It was warfare waged by the Malayan National Liberation Army (MNLA) and the military wing of the Malayan Communist Party (MCP) to gain independence from the British Empire. The colonial power referred to it as The Emergency, but the MNLA preferred to call it the Anti-British National Liberation War, and they were labeled as leftist guerrillas. During the bloody communist insurgency, over 31,000 Chinese Malayans were given a choice of either staying in prison or being deported to their ancestral homes in China to keep them from stirring up trouble in Malaya. Ah Sook was among those deported, but my father insisted that he was deported because of stealing not insurgency activities.

We never learned how my father came to have custody of all these children. Before my mother became his wife he arranged for the neighbors to look after the kids while he was at work and he rushed home in the evening to feed them. Over time this became too overwhelming for him and the neighbors persuaded him to remarry. These children called my mother Ah Yee or Auntie. When her own children came, we all followed suit and called her Ah Yee as well.

She told us very little about her early life with my father, but recalled the constant bombings during the war. She did not forgive him for not building a safe bomb shelter. She recounted with some envy how the neighbors had a concrete one built behind their house with proper steps leading into it while the shelter my father dug was just an open pit hidden ineffectively by some bananas leaves and overhanging branches of surrounding trees. During heavy bombings, shrapnel sliced through the succulent trunks of the banana trees and they landed dangerously close to the opening of the pit; there was nothing to prevent shells from falling straight into it and smashing everyone into smithereens. Once she saw a man injured by shrapnel and he continued to walk in a daze like a zombie.

Whenever she reminisced about the old days, we tried to get her to tell us about her early life as a bride. But she would abruptly close up like a clam and busy herself with her chores. No amount of coaxing and begging would draw her out of her shell. I could not fathom the terror she experienced having to spend her first night with a strange man.

In her bedroom was a heavily carved walnut wardrobe where she kept her trousseau: embroidered tablecloth, bed sheets, coverlets, and curtains which she only brought out on Chinese New Year to decorate the house, and garments she wore after the wedding ceremony, rich and resplendent with embroidery, sequins, and beads. While she was busy cooking in the kitchen, Kuan May and I stood in front of the full-length mirror and tried on her high-heeled shoes covered with delicate glass beads of light green leaves and pink flowers.

Weeks before Chinese New Year, Ah Yee prepared cakes and bought sweet delicacies from the shops. She cleaned the house from top to bottom, sweeping away any ill fortune to make room for incoming good luck for the New Year. She decorated the windows and doorframes with red paper-cutouts with couplets written by Fong in lavish gold or black in Chinese calligraphy of characters of happiness, wealth, and longevity.

My father claimed to be a Buddhist, but Kuan Yin, the Goddess of Mercy, was the main idol sitting atop the three-tier family altar, occupying a prominent place in the sitting room. The porcelain goddess with her kind smiling face, long Buddha ears, and hands poised in meditation, sat serenely on a lotus flower. A plate of Mandarin oranges and *gua zi* or watermelon seeds was always offered to her, and during the Chinese New Year celebration, the oranges were decorated with a band of serrated red paper. Below her was the ancestral altar with tablets of Chinese characters representing my father's deceased ancestors, incense and joss sticks burning in front of them. At the ground level was the Earth God, ensuring the earth remained fruitful. We were not farmers, but the tradition must have passed down to him.

On the kitchen wall next to Ah Yee's open stove was a small altar for the Kitchen God covered with soot and grime from the cooking. She offered him a special bowl of sweet, sticky, glutinous rice. He sat in the kitchen, a family gathering place, heard and saw everything that went on throughout the year. At the end of the year, he departed to heaven and gave an account on the household to the Heavenly God, the Jade Emperor. To prevent him from giving damaging reports, my mother sealed his mouth with the sticky rice and in case he could still talk, he would be so filled with its sweetness he would only remember to report on the good things about the family, ensuring we would be blessed with a favorable year.

The decorations at the altar from the previous year were taken down, burned a week before the New Year, and replaced with new bright red ones. Ah Yee burned fake gold and silver paper money which she spent hours folding into pyramidal ingot shapes, sending the Kitchen God together with Kuan Yin, the Earth God, and the ancestors with money in their pockets as bribes.

Our neighbors splurged and burned a golden chariot made of bamboo and paper with an entourage of paper figurines of servants, believing that the conflagration of such offerings transported them into the next world for their ancestors to use.

The lights were left on Chinese New Year's Eve, making the night as bright as day, an unheard-of extravagance. The house, the furniture, and the utensils were all spick and span. Ah Yee brought out her embroidered linen and curtains and hung them; they swayed in the breeze, ushering in a New Year. Before the stroke of midnight, she hid all the brooms and used a rag to sweep the floor, for the

Chinese believed that if a broom were used, all the good luck for the New Year would be swept away.

My parents allowed us to stay up late into this festive night. My father doted on Thye and she had a number of new dresses made and displayed them on hangers dangling from a clothesline in the veranda after she meticulously ironed out the wrinkles. Her fashion sense was imbued with sleek and slender elegance, waistline cinched with cummer-bunds or a wide sash to accentuate her shape, while under the skirts were extra-full crinoline petticoats, balancing the full bodice.

For Chinese New Year, Ah Yee sewed us new clothes, preferably red, the color for good luck. But most of the time, her tight budget only afforded her cheap remnants of leftover material in the market, and often they were not red. We wore our gold expandable bangles my father bought the girls when we were born. He was still working for the government and had a steady income. The first day of Chinese New Year was the only occasion we wore them. After that, Ah Yee carefully put them away under lock and key, afraid we would lose them through careless play.

On the rare occasions when her friends came to visit, she offered them F&N orange crush to drink, and *niangao*, the New Year cake, as a good-luck gift. Married guests gave âng-pau or red packets with coins and bills to the children. My father had no relatives living close by and Ah Yee was an orphan, so the few red packets we received from married adults warmed our pockets just for a little while.

Because Ah Yee had so many children, her friends had to give away a great number of red packets, so few of them came to visit. Instead, she took us to their homes, we were to behave ourselves and not forget to say *kam shieh*, thank you. Ah Yee's Tamil friend appeared on New Year without fail. Boon nicknamed her *Au Niah*, or black lady, because of her dark skin. She came to our house whenever there was food, especially when there was plenty of it. Being a Tamil, customs did not require her to give us any red packets. All day long, deafening firecrackers filled the air with smoke.

I was very fond of the paper-thin *kueh kapit* or love letter, a sweet crispy wafer made in a mold with intricate lace patterns, baked slowly over an open fire. Ah Yee bought them from a voluptuous Chinese woman, who bent over the fire, her full breasts barely contained in her *sarong*. The love letter was four inches across and was folded first in halves, then into quarters, resembling a folded lace handkerchief. I wondered how such a fat woman could churn out these delicate love letters.

On the fifteenth day of the Chinese New Year, *Chap Goh Meh*—the first full moon of the lunar calendar which also marked the last day of the New Year celebration—there were feastings and unending firing of crackers. In the city, the wealthy Chinese Associations sponsored operas performed amidst the burning of giant joss sticks, filling the air with their suffocating incense. Ah Yee served us bowls of glutinous rice flour balls, *tang yuan,* dyed in pink, blue, and yellow, all floating in a ginger-flavored syrupy soup. The flour balls were symbolic of family togetherness. Dinner was tender steamed chicken and rice cooked in fragrant anise.

After the celebration, she took down the embroidered curtains and linen, washed and put them away until the next Chinese New Year. Life was back to the mundane again. The brooms reappeared and the Kitchen God no longer received any special treatment except every day she continued to burn incense and joss sticks for him.

After my father finished his dinner, groggy from his big bottle of Tiger Beer or Guinness Stout, he went to sleep on his folding canvas recliner. We walked with Ah Yee to a local theater. She bought tickets for herself (and *Au Niah* when she came to visit) to watch a Chinese opera. Even if *Au Niah* was not around, there were no tickets for us. Having grown up in difficult times and deprived of most pleasures, Ah Yee was quite frugal, pinching pennies from her market money for this evening of luxury.

Many spectators who could not fork out the money to watch the opera stood on footstools craning their necks over the top of the wall to steal glimpses. Kuan May and I often squatted and squeezed in between their legs, only to be pushed rudely away by their feet. We moved to other less occupied and undesirable spots and watched through holes and cracks in the wooden wall until we grew tired, wandered around gawking at the hawkers cooking groundnuts in big steaming vats and drooling at displays of tempting, mouth-watering, sweet-and-sour pickled mangoes on skewers, fried legumes or steamed chickpeas, under the glaring fluorescent or kerosene lamps.

But our pockets were empty.

"*Chey, chey.*" The hawkers waved their arms, shooing us away as though we were pesky flies. Like street urchins, Kuan May and I walked away sucking on the hems of our dresses. The bright light from the different stalls cast our long shadows on the dirt lot, distorted by the uneven ground; two girls with long, skinny legs and enormous heads. The generators drowned out the mournful music streaming out of the theater. As the evening drew on, we grew sleepy, waited until Ah Yee came out of the theater with the crowd, and rounded us up. She spoke excitedly with *Au Niah* about the plot of the opera while *Au Niah* carried the littlest one, already fast asleep on her strong broad shoulders as we dragged our tired bodies homeward.

—

Ah Yee went down to Georgetown one hot afternoon. She returned with a new hairdo, an Italian short haircut with neat waves, still smelling of chemicals. From her shopping bag, she pulled out two dolls, a small, delicate, and intricately dressed doll for Kuan May and a big indestructible plastic one for me. Kuan May's doll had long curly blonde hair and her blue eyes closed when she lay down. Mine was a plump baby with clothes and shoes that could be removed. She had short curly dark brown hair, long lush eyelashes, and eyes that also closed when she was put to bed. This was the first time we had our own dolls. For the longest time, Kuan May and I had shared a doll with dirty curly brown hair and a ripped Victorian pinafore.

One sultry afternoon, a year before, while we were playing in the sand in the front yard, a Tamil Indian man selling hard candied groundnuts on a tray that he balanced on his turbaned head, and a folded wooden stand slung over his shoulders, walked by. Out of his *lungi*, he fished out an object, threw it close by us. We ran to pick it up. It was a doll. Her dress was a little dirty and torn but she had a sweet, smiling face. We both squealed with delight. The man turned around and smiled, pleased that we liked this unexpected present.

From another bag, Ah Yee took out a pair of maroon shoes and gave these to me. "Are these mine?" I asked. She nodded. This was the first time I had owned a pair of dressy shoes. Most days we ran around barefoot or wore flip-flops. I practiced walking in them.

Back in her bedroom, Ah Yee changed from her high-collared frogged-buttoned *sam foo* and pants to her airier *sarong,* pulling it up and draping it just above her breasts. Wearing her wooden clogs, she proceeded to the kitchen to warm up the dinner that she had prepared during lunch-time. That night Kuan May and I lay next to our dolls and my shoes still smelling of new leather. I drifted off to sleep with Kuan May telling me a bedtime story. Always she started with "Once upon a time..."

My father handed over most of his monthly wage to Ah Yee to run the household. She was able to afford some nice *nyonya kebaya,* and *sarong,* a traditional blouse-dress combination worn by women in Southeast Asia. Her gossamer blouses had intricate hand embroidery of flowers and vines and instead of buttons; they were held together with gold filigree decorative pins and chains. Most of the time she had on her ordinary cotton *batik sarong* while doing her chores and only topped that off with a flowery cotton blouse and pulled her *sarong* down to her waistline after she was done.

After Boon, my father wanted more baby boys to carry on the family name, but none came. The sixth was again a girl. In fact, she came too quickly for Ah Yee to go to the mater-nity hospital, lying on her bedroom floor in heavy labor. The neighbors sent Meng Kee into the village in a frantic search for the midwife. My father was at work.

Breathless, the midwife flew into the house, carrying a bag full of equipment. Curious, we followed close behind. She instructed Meng Kee to boil water and waved her hands to shoo us away. There followed a scurrying of activities between the kitchen and the bedroom; hot water and clean sheets were brought in. We heard a baby cry. In her hurry, the midwife left the door open a crack, and through it, I saw blood-stained sheets, the umbilical cord still attaching the baby to Ah Yee who lay quietly on the floor, spent. My father came flying home on his bike, wide-eyed and frightened, arriving just in time to hear the disappointing news, another cursed baby girl. My parents named her Wan, meaning cloud.

Ah Yee basked in the security of a well-provided household despite the size of her family. By then my adopted sisters were old enough to lend a hand in the washing, cooking, and babysitting of her growing brood of children.

One sultry afternoon, a rickshaw eked its way onto the sandy front walkway. Waves of oppressive heat rose from the tarmac road. Even the neighbors' dog was asleep in the cool screened porch, hardly bestirring itself with the arrival of the rickshaw and only raising one eyelid with disinterest. Kuan May and I were playing on the veranda. The rickshaw man pulled off the oil-cloth shade from the front of the seat and helped his lone passenger off. Through the rising heat, a heavy-set woman clambered off with a great deal of difficulty, her *batik sarong* getting caught on the metal straps of the vehicle. She had on a *nyonya kebaya* of thin transparent linen with embroidered edges, her wispy white hair pulled up in a small bun held together with a few long pins. She wore a pair of wooden clogs and held a shoulder bag close to her chest. Excitedly, we ran inside to tell Ah Yee we had a visitor.

Ah Yee walked to the front door, balancing baby Wan on her hip. A gnarled old bougainvillea bush framed the porch door, profuse fuchsia blossoms cascading from the branches. There was hardly a breath of breeze. Instantly Ah Yee recognized her aunt. Her heart must have skipped a beat. Her aunt stopped her slow shuffle and began to cry, reaching her free hand toward Ah Yee, who right away commanded us to help her. Kuan May and I held her sweaty, lumpy body on each side as she walked slowly toward the house. The rickshaw man wanted to know whether he should wait for her. She turned to him and said, "Yes." Whereupon he quickly withdrew into the dark, cool interior of the rickshaw and pulled the shade to take a snooze.

When her aunt plopped into an easy chair in the sitting room, Ah Yee scurried around to serve her some refreshment. With her roving eyes, her aunt surveyed the room, peering at the china and linen in the glass cabinet and commenting on Ah Yee's good fortune, *"Lueh chiak pa, eoh kha."* You will have a full belly and spend your time shaking your legs, meaning Ah Yee would live a comfortable life. She waved her fat hand in our direction, indicating we would care for Ah Yee in her old age. She bemoaned the fact that her daughters, after being married off, neglected her, leaving her alone to fend for herself. Tears flowed freely down her puffy cheeks, caught up in the furrows of her heavy jowls which betrayed traces of meanness, greed, and cruelty carved over the years.

We milled around, looking at her with curious eyes but mainly hoping she would not drink the F&N orange crush or eat the Marie biscuits. No such luck, she reached out with her fat fingers, ate and drank.

Ah Yee seemed uncomfortable and ill at ease in front of her, rocking Wan on her hip, and running her tongue sideways between her teeth, chewing it. Her aunt blew her nose noisily into her cambric handkerchief. She wanted Ah Yee to know she had always had her welfare in mind. The fact that she was now basking in the richness of life was ample proof her aunt was right all along to match her to my father, despite his age.

It soon became obvious where she was heading. She had come upon hard times, and needed some money. Naturally, she turned to Ah Yee. Of course, she would only borrow from her. In due time she would pay her back. Ah Yee knew better. She sent her off in the same rickshaw armed with some cash after she paid the fare. This would not be the last time we saw her aunt; she became a regular visitor to our house on the same errand of needs and wants. In time, her visits did not draw any more curiosity from us. We ran into the house to announce to Ah Yee that her evil aunt had come again.

In the cool evenings when the soft sea breeze blew gently, it was Ah Yee's time to relax after a hectic day. We went *makan angin,* literally eat wind in Malay, taking leisurely strolls down River Road along the fence of the Tamil Girls' School across from our house toward the sundry shop next to Sungai Pinang.

When I was five years old, during one of those walks, I said, "I will not get married when I grow up."

My mother chastised me. I did not tell her then I could not envision living a life like hers, overburdened with children. Deep down, I felt there was a spirit in me that needed to be released, to be free to choose.

5

My brother Boon, the carrier of my father's family name

For as long as I can remember my brother Boon was the apple of my parents' eye. My adopted brother, Ah Wee, did not factor in as the true carrier of my father's family name since he was not from his bloodline. Boon, being the only carrier of the Lai family name, was free to do what he fancied.

Boon had afternoon school and spent his mornings exploring the estuary a mile from the house, even though he was strictly forbidden to do so. The boys from the neighborhood usually got together in the early steaming morning and waded in the muddy water barefoot, looking for any living creatures stranded by the receding tides. There were plenty of scrambling and scurrying small crabs and occasionally fish flapping in the mud. Kuan May and I were barred from joining them.

Once in a while, out of curiosity and boredom, we followed from a distance, hitching up our skirts so they would not be caked with mud. The heat and humidity soon became intolerable, beads of sweats glistened on the boys' backs. The rotten egg stench from the estuary wafted to our nostrils, and the tenacious mud clung to our flip-flops, making a sucking noise as we tried to release them from its hold. We took them off and wriggled our feet in the luxuriously soft mud. Invariably, Boon spotted us.

"Ugh, girls! Why do you have to follow us?"

At first, he was mad, but we promised not to tell Ah Yee about his forbidden exploration in the river. He threw his hands in the air and resigned to let us follow his gang. It was rumored there were *buaya*—crocodiles—in the river. We had never seen them, though one of the kids claimed to have spotted one close to the sundry shop resting in one of the holes in the rocky embankment, basking in the after-noon sun.

On one of those days of river exploration, one of the boys stepped on a piece of broken glass. Bright red blood gushed from his foot, mixing with the glistening black mud. Boon picked him up and placed him on the marshy grass, pressing hard with his fingers to staunch the bleeding. He wrapped the foot with a piece of material torn from his shirt. The cut was deep but it finally stopped bleeding. Somehow, Ah Yee got wind of it and Boon's carefree days in the river were over, at least until he could sneak his way there again. Yet he never felt the sting of punishment for it, only the bite of her words.

On weekdays, Ah Yee sent Kuan May and me to look for Boon when it was close to lunchtime to get him ready for school at the Pyket Methodist Boys' School. He bathed, dressed, and ate lunch. His uniform was all white—shorts, shirt, socks, and canvas shoes. She combed his hair with a generous glob of Brylcreem, smoothed down the recalcitrant strands, and plastered them on the side of his head, transforming him from a mud-covered urchin to a meek-looking schoolboy. She took him on her bicycle, making a shortcut through a village on a dirt road strewn with pebbles and sharp rocks. One day, they never made it to school. Distracted by Thye waving at her, Ah Yee's bike stumbled over a rock. They fell, sustained cuts and bruises. And she lost her front teeth, spattering Boon's white uniform with blood. She struggled home with him wailing on the bike.

Boon was older than most of the boys in the neighborhood except Meng Chai, the only male child of our Cantonese neighbors, a frail, etiolated boy whose pallor reflected his mother's effort of shielding him from the full glare of the sun, only letting him outside in the evening. So, Boon became the default leader. His daily dose of the tropical sun made him so tanned he could easily pass as a Malay boy. Meng Chai's bony face and lanky frame echoed the sinuosity of the seedling of a pale bean sprout desperately seeking the sun.

When he was in a good mood, Boon let Kuan May and me follow him and the boys into the dark, dense, cool woods next to the Tamil Girls' School in search of black spiders hiding in the spiny sisal bushes. We kept them in matchboxes lined with spiny leaves. Then we returned to our veranda and had a spider fight. My spiders were always considered inferior, but it all changed when Kuan May caught the mother of all spiders. It defeated several of the boys' spiders which quivered and retreated into the deeper recesses of the spiny leaves instead of fighting her gigantic spider. The boys then viewed her in a different light. They begged to trade her spider with their precious possessions—the much-coveted, shiny, variegated marbles. She stood her ground and refused. Her spider finally languished in the matchbox and died.

When I was five, Thye quit school. Ah Yee made her take care of her babies, rocking them to sleep as she sang them lullabies. One day she entered a singing contest and it was broadcast over the local radio, the Rediffusion. We glued our ears to the radio, listening to her. Her voice squeaked when she hit a high note at the end of her song; she turned red when she heard it. Nevertheless, she won a consolation prize and was awarded a can of Milo. She was so proud of it she refused to open it to make drinks despite our constant pleading. The can stood temptingly on top of the cupboard in the kitchen, daring us to open it. Believing she was going to be a famous singer, she practiced incessantly, *do re mi fa so la ti*, trying her best to hit the high note.

Boon was the first one to succumb to temptation on that drizzly cold afternoon when he, Kuan May, and I were cooped up in the house with nothing else to do, an afternoon that called for a warm Milo drink. None of his friends was out looking for him to play. Ah Yee was resting in bed nursing the baby. He waited till Thye went to take her bucket bath, then hoisted me onto his shoulders so I could bring down the can of Milo. He pried open the metal cap, revealing an aluminum seal which when broken and peeled off would reveal our crime. Boon hesitated just a little and then tore the seal off. Each of us took a heaping spoonful of Milo powder and shoved it into our mouths, not daring to tempt fate by making a cup of Milo using Ah Yee's thermos of hot water.

While we were enjoying the Milo powder, Meng Chai, the boy next door, saw us through the mesh screen of the kitchen and instinctively knew we were up to no good. He quickly sounded the alarm, and we heard Thye's voice from the bathroom warning us not to touch her Milo. Hurriedly Boon picked me up to put the can back, we ran through the kitchen and made our getaway by the back door. He carried me on his back, and I bobbed up and down as we ran across the field, past Ahmadkan's house toward the government mansions where the Eurasians lived. There we waited with no particular plan.

Time crawled. With nothing else to do, we milled outside the hedges of one of the mansions trying to peek at the goings-on in the yard. Except for a gardener working outside, the place was quiet. The rain had long stopped and the bright tropical sun shone. The humidity intensified and steam rose from the grass in the field. Staying in the shade, we dangled our legs into the deep drains which surrounded the mansion just outside the ixora hedges, picking clovers, chewing on them, and sucking sweet nectar from the red ixora flowers. The afternoon dragged on and we became bored, wondering whether it was all worth our while stealing a few spoonfuls of Milo, by now its taste a distant memory.

We had no allowances and could only drool over the display of sweets and biscuits in the sundry shop. Some days Kuan May and I stood in front of the shop like a pair of ragamuffins, chewing on the edges of our dresses until the shopkeeper shooed us away. We left the mansions and scoured the neighborhood for tin cans, empty toothpaste tubes, tin foils, and brought these to an old Chinese man who stationed himself under a bridge by the river, spidery wrinkles crawling all over his face. He owned two baskets of junk which he carried between his shoulders using a long pole. He never said a word when we brought him the recycled stuff, dutifully weighing them before slipping some coins into our palms.

We scampered away to the sundry shop, making our journey more exciting by crossing the river on the gigantic metal sewage pipe, hot from being baked in the sun, instead of using the pedestrian bridge. High up on the sewage pipe with no guardrails to prevent us from plunging into the raging, muddy river twenty feet below, perhaps to our death or to be devoured by the crocodiles—if they truly existed— the death-defying act gave me a sense of exhilaration and freedom. I thought if I fell, the river would sweep me right into the Strait of Penang. Who knew where fate would bring me then, perhaps into the vast Indian Ocean? With my arms outstretched, balancing precariously on top of the pipe, and the wind blowing, for a brief moment I imagined I could take off and fly.

Ah Yee's calling us for supper woke me from my reverie. We dragged our reluctant bodies back to the house, feeling very guilty. Thye had long discovered her precious can of Milo had been pillaged and she was not the first to taste the fruits of her labor. She had wanted to show her gleaming prize to my father before it was opened. We slunk guiltily into the kitchen, feeling sick to our stomachs. In the heat of her temper, she flung the can across the room, spilling most of the Milo all over the floor. Ah Yee yelled at her for wasting it, but Thye did not care. Her eyes were swollen from crying. She knew Boon was the culprit, and she screamed at him. Kuan May and I stood stock still. My father tried to console her, telling her it was only a can of Milo. But he was wrong. To her it was a sign of her great success as a singer, a trophy won with a great deal of courage and pluck.

I was sure my father would dish out his punishment, but he dismissed the whole incident with a wave of his hand, leaving Thye with her vague veiled threats of reporting the incident to her boyfriend when Boon would surely be in deep trouble. She left the kitchen in a huff, stamping her feet and retreating to our shared bedroom, crying her eyes out.

I realized then if it had been one of the girls and not Boon who'd committed the act, my father would have been angrier and the result would have been vastly different. His precious bearer of the family name could do no wrong. Even if he did, he was readily forgiven.

That evening, I did not have much of an appetite. In some way, I felt worse than if I had been physically punished.

6

The color of our skin

In truth, other than the *Orang Asli*, the indigenous people, and the national minority of Peninsular Malaya, we, the other inhabitants, are immigrants with no claim to be the original people of Malaya. Yet, as a child I always felt there was a constant tension among the neighbors in our small River Road community—the Chinese, the Malays, the Indians, and the Eurasians—as to who was on top of the pecking order. To be sure some, like the Tamil Indians, had already accepted their fate at the bottom of the social hierarchy.

At River Road, the government owned all the houses including the mansions occupied by the Eurasians. Ahmadkan's house and the Malay houses were the exceptions. There was a distinct hierarchy in the housing assigned to the government civil servants. The Tamil Indians lived in rows of small cement block homes just beyond the bushes at the back of our house; four of their homes could easily fit into ours. A deep and wide monsoon drain separated our homes from theirs and only a concrete bridge connected our two worlds. There were no guardrails to prevent the Indian children from falling into the gigantic drains filled with fast-flowing water during the monsoon season. They were always playing next to them; there was a dearth of play areas near their houses, and for some miraculous reason their parents were not concerned at all.

Two Malay and two Chinese families lived in a row of terraced housing with four big and comfortable homes. My father, as a switchgear inspector for the National Electric Department, was assigned one of them. We were one of the two Chinese families. There were two bedrooms, a big wrought iron bed was in each of them; all eight of us children squeezed into the first bedroom, either sprawling on the bed or on the floor. Situated to the right of Ahmadkan's house were several huge mansions meant for the higher-ranking government officials, many of whom were Eurasians.

Our house was clearly better than the cement block homes of the Indians but could not be compared to the mansions. This kind of housing assignment insidiously instilled in my young mind that the Eurasians were somehow superior to us in the ordinary government quarters. The size of our quarters, and the fact that they were equipped with running water and electricity, elevated the importance of our status above the Indian laborers.

Tall hedges of ixora and hibiscus blocked my view of the mansions; I could only catch glimpses of the second-floor balconies caressed by the feathery leaves of the rain and flame of the forest trees. The occupants were rarely seen, always chauffeured in government cars with tinted windows. The children never mixed with the likes of us. On rare evenings when I ran into them *makan angin*, taking a leisurely stroll, there was no friendly greeting of *jiak pa boey*, the island's greeting of "have you eaten" or any hint of acknowledgment of my existence. They simply walked on as though I was invisible. The tall hedges separated them from the rest of the world, but they needed the people in the lower rung of society in their daily lives: an *amah* to care for the little ones, and wash their clothes, a cook to prepare their meals, and scrub their pots and pans in the outdoor ; a gardener to clip the bushes and care for the grounds. Oftentimes, when a gardener spotted Kuan May and me, he chased us away, waving his menacing clippers. His association with these higher officials seemed to elevate, at least in his mind, his status.

Likewise, we, living in the ordinary government quarters, did not mix or play with the Indian children. Although there were no tall hedges to separate us, there was the wide and deep monsoon drain forming a big unspoken divide between our two worlds. I often stood on our side of the monsoon drain peering into their world, curious about their way of life.

The Indian mothers let their children run wild, wearing only an *aranjanma,* a girdle-like thread ornament, sometimes with a talisman dangling over their protruding bellies. They waded in the mud, barefoot, and then traipsed into their houses, with tiny solitary windows scarcely letting any light into the interior, dark and gloomy even in broad daylight. They had no electricity, even though many of the Indians worked for the electricity department. They lit dim kerosene lamps at night.

In some ways, the hierarchy also reflected the color of our skin. The dark-skinned labored in the sun whereas the fair-complexioned officials worked in the offices, sheltered from it. Many of the Chinese came to the Malayan Peninsula to work in the tin mines and the rubber plantations as laborers and the ports as porters, saving their meager earnings for their future generations, after paying for their three bowls of rice. A number of them succeeded in amassing a fortune that enabled them to become *towkays*, owning shops in Georgetown, climbing up the social ladder. Their stores occupied the ground floor and their families lived on the second floor. They owned their homes, whereas my father lived in a government-owned house. A small number of them became so rich that they were able to build rows of houses to keep generations of extended families living under one roof. Wealthy Chinese clans banded together to form associations, such as the Khoo or the Lim *Kong Si*. My father was a Hakka from a guest family; he would never achieve such social status. We remained outsiders from any associations.

Tamil Indians from South India, immigrant laborers imported under the East Indian British Company during the British colonial days, had extremely dark skin. The Malays had brown skin in between that of the Chinese and the Indians. European colonization of vast swathes of Southeast Asia for several hundred years led to the burgeoning of Eurasians. Although their complexion was not that much lighter than the Malays, the fact that they were of mixed European and Asian blood somehow placed them higher. Their great asset was their command of and fluency in the Queen's English, a requirement for higher office in the government sector. Behind their backs, the Chinese called them half-caste. This social hierarchy seemed to have endowed us with a sense of superiority over the Tamil Indians even while we knew we were at a lower social rung than the Eurasians.

In our backyard, a *jambu-ayer* tree bore abundant juicy fruits, so many, it was impossible for us to eat them all. Many fell to the ground, luring the timid, hungry, barefoot Indian children to venture into our yard to collect them. The girls gathered the fruits in their dirty skirts while the boys filled their underwear, bulging with the stolen goods, baring their dark bottoms. Kuan May and I stormed out of the screen door, yelling and shooing them away, scaring the chickens. The boys lost most of their loot in their hasty retreat. Ah Yee did not reprimand us when we played such monstrous tricks on them; she had not given them any slack when they wandered into our yard, an inherent racial bias that seeped insidiously into our young, formative subconscious minds.

Kuan May preferred the company of Meng Ling, my neighbors' youngest daughter, and only played with me when Meng Ling's mother did not invite Kuan May over. She described the dolls and toys Meng Ling owned, making me intensely jealous, while I spent the day alone and bored. Once, Ah Yee took us to a cinema and I sat next to two girls close to my age, clothed in beautiful frilly dresses, chatting merrily away while licking lollipops. My rough cotton dress could not be compared with theirs. I tried to catch their attention but the girl sitting closer to me stuck her tongue at me and gave me the *juling mata,* spiteful stare. I was so desperate to make friends I paid no heed to the movie. When it ended, I followed them, longing for a token of friendship. Back home, I lied to Kuan May that I had made two friends and for days I hoped they would miraculously show up to play with me, but no one ever did. For some time afterward, I pretended to play with my imaginary friends, talking to them as though they were there with me.

Kuan May and I had not started primary school and so we had plenty of time to kill. I followed her lead as she was older and Ah Yee always blamed her when one of our escapades went awry. The Tamil school was across the street from our house, bordered on one side by the Sungai Pinang. The school boasted a well-kept ground with the flame of the forest and frangipani trees, all fenced in with barbwire and surrounded by a deep trench. The groundskeeper did not allow other children to play there, and the more we were forbidden from entering the inviting, spacious grassy field, the more it beckoned to us.

The only time we went there without being chased away was when the girls performed an Indian dance on stage in their colorful *sari*. Boon walked up boldly on the long driveway leading to the main entrance of the school; we followed timidly behind, watching closely for the groundskeeper. At the school entrance, pink and white periwinkles grew in a garden bordered by rocks painted with white lime. The groundskeeper sat on the stone steps of the veranda with his *lungi* rolled up. Our instinct was to run, but he just stared, did not shout or get up to chase us away.

With their hair braided and wrapped around their heads, tied with bright red ribbons and adorned with blood-red hibiscus, the Tamil Indian girls sang, hitting two bamboo sticks together as they danced. They had powdered their faces white with *bedak sejuk*, rice-powder paste, lined their eyes with black kohl, and painted their hands with henna.

Wearing their school uniform of white blouses and long blue skirts, their feet were bare except for rings on their toes. A Westerner, a blond-haired artist, sat in front of a huge easel, directly below the stage, painting them. He was the first white man I had ever seen. The girls came to life on his canvas. Several times, he asked them to pose and they stood poised with their sticks in the air.

—

One afternoon, Kuan May and I lingered outside the school fence, picking wild passion fruits growing on vines and popping them into our mouths. The sweet and sour juice and seeds awakened our taste buds. We plucked the pods of *buah petai* from a clump of trees, sat on the grass under the shade peeling and eating the pungent flat beans, paying for it the next day with bloated bellies troubled with foul-smelling flatulence.

The groundskeeper left the school on his bicycle. He wore a white *haji songkok* which meant he had made the pilgrimage to Mecca. This was our chance to get in. As soon as he was out of sight, Kuan May and I crossed the street and leaped over the trench. I almost lost my footing, my body leaning dangerously backward. Kuan May had already reached the fence, lifted the lowest rung of the wires, and motioned for me to hurry up. I crawled under on my belly and reached the forbidden land. She followed suit as I lifted the barbwire for her.

Elated, we ran toward the flame trees. Big, elongated, brown pods covered the ground. We broke them apart looking for the waxy red seeds lining the inside neatly like rows of soldiers standing at attention. We filled our pockets with the beads and dared each other to put the tiny red seeds into our nostrils despite Ah Yee's warning that they could get stuck and we would end up in the hospital to have our noses cut open. When we grew tired of that, we climbed up the *ramat emas* trees to pick their bright yellow trumpet flowers. I was two-thirds of the way up when I heard Kuan May cry, "He is back!"

My heart raced, I slid down the tree, scraping my belly. Kuan May was already out of the fence waving for me to run. He spotted us. As I slipped under the barbwire, it snared my best frilly dress and I heard it tear. Blood from my scraped belly had already seeped through the bodice. The grounds-keeper jumped off his bike, threw it down beside the road, and raced toward us. I could feel his breath as I jumped over the trench. I had seen him spank trespassers.

Across the street we ran. Kuan May yelled at me to run away from our home; she did not want to let him know where we lived. I turned my head as I ran. He held onto his *lungi*, swearing.

Later in the day, I sat on our bedroom floor while Kuan May cleaned my wound with iodine. It burned. Ah Yee happened to peek in and scolded us for being tomboys. My belly still bears a half-inch scar from that afternoon's misadventure.

Days passed. We pondered how best to take our revenge. While the Tamil children were in school, Kuan May implemented her plan.

In the early afternoon, the groundskeeper rang the dismissal bell. Droves of noisy and hungry children rushed down the road. We lay on our bellies in the tall grass in the field, hidden from view. Our first victim picked up a package and opened it, took out a black ball, and placed it in her mouth. She spat it out and threw the whole package away in disgust. More children, unaware of her kismet fell prey to our tricks. By then we were rolling on the grass, curling up into balls, and roaring with laughter. We had collected goat droppings, wrapping them into small neat packages and placing them by the roadside. The droppings were not hard to find since goatherds shepherded their goats by our front yard every morning and evening. Older Tamil children began to give chase, like cowards, we ran into the house howling. Ah Yee was taking her afternoon nap with her baby and was unaware of our antics.

One evening, Meng Chai brought over a plastic model of human poop. He and Ah Wee boldly crossed the monsoon drain to the Tamil territory where several naked children squatted on the cement walkway, aiming their bare butts at the drain, pooping. Meng Chai surreptitiously placed his poop model on the walkway close to a squatting Tamil kid. The kid's mother came out and yelled at him for pooping on the walkway instead of into the monsoon drain. She went into the house and came out with a bucket and a coconut frond broomstick. By then Meng Chai had picked up the model and walked back to his side of the monsoon drain. When she did not find the poop, she was bewildered. Meng Chai replaced the model on the walkway as soon as she went back into the house. She whacked her child on the head when she returned to see the poop on the walkway again. Emerging the second time with the bucket and broomstick, the poop model had again disappeared. Then she spotted the two Chinese boys giggling from across the monsoon drain. Putting down her bucket, she picked up the ends of her *sari* and ran after them, waving her broomstick, her hair unraveling from her bun. Crossing the monsoon drain briefly, she stopped abruptly as though there were invisible barriers barring her from stepping over the line that divided our worlds.

In those days in our neighborhood, there were no flush toilets. Our very own squatting toilet was at the back of the kitchen but the Tamil Indians had to contend with mephitic pit latrines in communal outhouses. Buckets were placed at the bottom of the holes of the squatting toilets to catch the waste which a Chinese night soil man emptied weekly in the early evenings when the temperature had cooled down, filling the air with the stench of human waste. Unfortunately, it was also when most people had dinner. He carried two big wooden buckets hanging from a flexible wooden pole slung over his shoulders. Wooden lids were loosely held to the buckets with ropes, as he made his way from outhouse to outhouse. Brown and muscular, he wore only a dark loincloth with a towel around his waist and on his feet, tire sandals. He wore no mask and yet he did not seem to be overcome by the smell. Periodically he stopped and put down his stinking buckets, pulled out a dirty gray towel to mop his forehead, his tanned back glistened with sweat.

Children mocked him as though he was responsible for the stench. The dogs barked and chased after him, attempting to nip at his heels. Kuan May and I were not different from the other children, we let him know what a stink he made, *"Chhau sai,"* until one day he dropped his buckets and gave chase. We ran into the house and hid in our bedroom, peering through the curtains. He stopped short of the doorstep of our front porch and yelled back that we made the stink.

Once, Kuan May and I held our noses and walked close to him. This made him hopping mad. He set down his buckets with such vigor that one of the lids came off, revealing numerous white wriggling maggots, creatures the size of rice grains. I lost my appetite for dinner. For days afterward, I could not bring myself to eat rice, leaving most of the grains on the plate, never mind if I ended up marrying a husband with horrible pockmarks on his face.

Ah Yee made us pick our plates clean, not because of the poor starving children in China, but because, if we left bits of rice on them, we would be cursed with pockmarked husbands and our children would be scarred for life.

Lau peh mor peng,
Kniar tiow teng.

A pock-marked father,
scar-faced offspring.

After that incident, I was remorseful and wondered how the night soil man's wife and children could withstand the smell he brought home with him every day. Why would he want this job, the lowliest of occupations one could imagine?

One evening, as I sat in the kitchen eating my dinner at the high table by myself after a late afternoon nap, a whiff of excrement wafted by. Through the wire mesh of the screen I spotted the night soil man swinging his buckets. I did not hop down to tease him.

—

We were not close to the two Malay families who lived in the same row of terraced housing as us. One day Fong and Boon started a fight with the Malay children living in the last house. None of the parents were home. Someone threw a pebble, and then World War III erupted with stones pelting down like hail. Kuan May and I were Fong and Boon's reinforcement and collected more stones for their ammunition; the war escalated. Then Boon threw a huge rock onto their kitchen roof; a loud crack was followed by shattering of glass. The Malay children made a hasty retreat indoors with one of them limping. When Ah Yee returned from the market, she was none too thrilled. My parents made Fong and Boon climb up the neighbor's roof via a drainpipe to fix the hole in the roof with tar.

The other Chinese family in this complex were our immediate neighbors—Meng Chai and Meng Ling's family. Their home was sandwiched between two houses, dark and gloomy. His father parked his motorcycle in the long hallway. He had two wives.

All afternoon and evening, the two wives often sat on the front veranda with one leg tugged under their buttocks and the other pulled up to their chins, fanning themselves from the heat with palm fans, gossiping about their neighbors. The first wife chattered incessantly while the second merely listened and nodded in agreement. They spoke Cantonese, not the island's dialect of Hokkien. They cracked watermelon seeds deftly between their teeth, spit the shells on the floor, and fished the kernel with their tongues like a mosquito snaring its victim. Chickens swarmed around their feet, pecking at the husks, hoping to find any remnants of kernel missed by the women's acrobatic tongues.

Meng Ling's mother, the first wife, behaved as though she was a cut above us, looking down on Ah Yee, a young woman married to an older man, a widower. She considered Ah Yee our *amah* and despised her for losing control of her children, letting us run wild morning, day, and night, exposing ourselves to the hot sun, darkening our skin. To her, we were no better than the Tamil children living beyond the monsoon drain.

In Asia, fair skin connoted the leisure class; only laborers worked and baked in the sun. Our darker complexion placed us several notches below the first wife's preconceived notion of social status. She shunned us and forbade her children to play with us without her permission.

Meng Ling was forbidden to play outside, kept away from the sun and from us. Sometimes she begged her mother to let her play with us, and on rare occasions, her mother acceded to her request and called Kuan May over while I was left standing outside, salivating like a dog. We knew she said bad things about us because the wall separating our houses was thin. She did not realize that having grown up next door, listening to her for as long as we could remember, we understood every insulting word she uttered.

One sultry afternoon, a traveling dentist came, carrying his equipment in a case slung over his shoulder. The first wife had a rotten tooth that had been plaguing her and she often sat on the front veranda holding her jaw. The sight of the traveling dentist was a relief for her; she beckoned him to come. He put his equipment down and set up a tall folding chair right in their front yard. We scrambled to have a good look, but she shooed us away. We tiptoed our way back. The dentist told her the tooth needed to come out. She haggled over the fee. He numbed the area with salve, waited, and used a pair of pliers to yank it out as she let out a series of cries. Blood oozed from her mouth, and he stopped the bleeding by having her bite on a piece of gauze. With that in her mouth, it was hard for her to yell at us as we gawked at her. He cleaned his medieval instruments, packed up, and was soon on his way.

Mei Mei was the older sister of Meng Chai and Meng Ling. She was seventeen years old, the age when Ah Yee was sent away to marry. While Meng Ling was pampered and never had to do any household work, Mei Mei did heavy chores including cleaning, cooking, washing, ironing, and running errands on the bicycle. She rode to the wet market every day, braving the intense sun to buy food for the family. She also sent the family's linen to the Indian *dhobi*, a laundryman at the *dhobi ghat*. She grew darker by the day.

A banyan tree with its spreading leaves and aerial roots and a huge hole in the trunk big enough to let us play hide and seek, sat directly in front of the fourth house in the terraced housing. Black scarred markings just above the hole looked like a pair of watchful eyes under a wrinkled forehead. Superstitious Chinese put up a small altar inside the hole, believing a spirit lived in the tree. People began to burn incense and bring offerings of fruits and cakes. One evening, my father sent me to the sundry shop to buy a bottle of Guinness Stout. On my way home, I passed by the banyan tree, heart thumping in my chest. The light was fast fading. Two shadowy figures whispered. Panicked, I raced past them and caught a glimpse of Mei Mei with the taller shadow holding her close, speaking in Tamil. Confused, I ran home and handed the Guinness Stout to my father. He stared at me with his heavy-lidded eyes and said in his raspy voice, "Did you just see a ghost?"

One evening I ventured farther afield from our home and crossed a big bridge to Georgetown proper. I caught sight of Mei Mei and the dark *dhobi*, leaning on the bridge, holding hands, whispering to each other as they looked wistfully over Sungai Pinang. The sun sent its last lingering orange rays over its smooth satiny surface.

Sometime later, through the thin wall that separated our two houses, we heard the first wife yelling at Mei Mei in Cantonese *"Lei geh chau hai lang ah?Pok gai."* Your pussy is pretty? Go to hell. She called her a loose woman, a dishrag, a whore! Pots and pans clattered on the cement floor of the kitchen, a broom flew out of the house. We tumbled outside to watch. Mei Mei struggled to get her hair out of the first wife's fists. Ah Yee came to intervene, *"Hoe sim."* Have a heart. But the first wife chased her away. *"Pat phor."* Busybody. Telling her to mind her own business and her own bunch of wild children.

From that day on, the first wife no longer sent Mei Mei out to the market or to the *dhobi ghat*. Instead riding her bicycle with a basket on the handlebar, her enormous bottom spread over the narrow seat, straining against her weight. She locked Mei Mei in the house, the key to Mei Mei's freedom worn on her thick waist.

Then one day, Mei Mei vanished. Meng Chai's father came flying home on his motorcycle. They searched high and low for her, even venturing to the Tamils' quarters, but they never once went to the Eurasians' to look for her. The first wife was too proud to ask us for help, but we combed the neighborhood, going as far as the bridge where I once saw Mei Mei talking with the *dhobi*. There was no sign of her.

A few days later we heard the news: Mei Mei had eloped with the *dhobi*. It was a double blow for the first wife, an elopement and with a Tamil man to boot. Mei Mei disgraced the family; she would never be allowed to set foot in the house again. Fairness of complexion was revered among those with darker skin; it was not difficult for the Tamil Indians to accept this fair maiden into their midst. The *dhobi* stole Mei Mei's heart; she married him and helped him with the laundry. She coiled her long black hair into a bun. On her forehead, she proudly wore a *bindi*.

The ongoing undercurrent of the class struggles in our community and the way the adults behaved toward the other racial groups played a role in how we children learned to relate to the other races, not with tolerance, kindness, or respect but with callousness, cruelty, and disdain. Even as I watched and learned from my mother's uncharitable treatment of the Tamil children, I was heartened by Mei Mei's love story. She dared to defy her mother's prejudice against the darker members of our small community, leaving her familiar home albeit a loveless one, to venture into a world far different from hers. Her love and courage transcended the racial divide.

Passing the banyan tree again one evening, Mei Mei's brave and decisive act caused me to pause and think: When it came time for me to choose my own fate, would I have her grit and spunk to buck convention and follow my heart for what was right for me?

7
My father's retirement

The only photograph of my father on the job pictured him perched high on an electrical pole with a group of Tamil Indians, wearing his pith helmet, white polo shirt, and wide-legged khaki shorts. He spoke fluent Tamil. Whenever he biked through the Indian village, he was hailed with greetings in Tamil and the entire village seemed to know him. On payday, a man from the city council set up a table in the compound under the shade of the spreading almond tree in front of our row of terraced housing. He had a ledger and next to him were piles of brown envelopes with stamps bearing the picture of Queen Elizabeth II while all the laborers and my father lined up to sign for their pay.

As children, we ate dinner before he came home; there were too many of us to fit at the table. None of us wished to have dinner with him. The unfortunate soul who over-slept her afternoon nap ate with him and had to bear the brunt of his constant grumbling on how useless we girls were. Blaming Ah Yee for the failings of her daughters, he only claimed them as his if they accomplished something great, which was not often. Ah Yee kept him company while he ate, rarely uttering a word. After dinner, he lay on his canvas lounger out on the porch in his white cotton singlet and blue-and-white checked *sarong*, smoking a cigar or a pipe, looking quite content. By then he was sufficiently groggy from his drinks, and we knew to stay out of his way.

He was a stern man of few words, except when he was angry. His parents had migrated from Guangzhou Province in the southern part of China to Singapore, a British Straits Settlement. None of us knew what his parents did or how my father had come to reside in Penang, another British Straits Settlement, while his older brother lived in Kuala Lumpur, which later became the capital of Malaya.

He did not tell us about his role in the war, and we were too afraid to ask. We avoided him at all costs. When he walked into a room, he seemed to suck the joy out of it. We stopped our frivolous play and kept quiet. Sometimes while he was playing solitaire, he allowed us to pluck his white hair until he grew tired and roughly brushed us off.

In the ornately carved walnut cupboard in the sitting room, which probably came as a set with Ah Yee's wardrobe, was evidence of his having been in the British army: his khaki uniform, pith helmet, and a rifle. Ah Yee said the Japs had taken him in for questioning and they had subjected him to Chinese water torture: forcing water down his throat into his stomach and stomping on his abdomen. We found a book on *Learn to Speak Japanese—arigato, sayonara*. Indeed, most people of my father's generation spoke rudimentary Japanese.

He owned a Victrola gramophone and collected many records from the 1920s to the 1940s. We could still make it play by cranking it up manually and listening to the scratchy and mournful sounds of his records when we were bored with nothing else to do.

Oh Rose Marie I love you
I'm always dreaming of you
No matter what I do I can't forget you
Sometimes I wish that I'd never met you
And yet if I should lose you
T'would mean my very life to me
Of all the queens that ever lived I'd choose you
To rule me my Rose Marie

The mournful sounds came through the horn of the gramophone, which had a picture of a terrier cocking his ear listening.

We were not sure whether he went to school, but he picked up some words of English while serving under the British. Some nights when he was inebriated and his eyes were glazed over, he would complain about how useless his children were in his broken English, putting the blame squarely on Ah Yee's shoulders, forgetting all the while she did not understand a word. We kept our mouths shut and stayed out of sight, not wishing to incite his unreasonable and unpredictable anger.

One day when he biked home from work, a cat followed him. When he got off, it began to rub against his legs, looked at him, and meowed. We had no pets, and Ah Yee had no use for them; they would just be extra mouths to feed. Kuan May and I begged him to let us keep it. He was in a good mood and said it could stay. When morning came, it was nowhere to be seen. Ah Yee said my father had taken the cat with him. I had a hunch he had dropped it off far away from our home. Worse, I feared he would have had no qualms about drowning it in the Sungai Pinang.

On *Qingming* or Tomb-Sweeping Day one April morning, my father arranged for the children to be carried on the few bicycles we owned to go to Mount Erskine in Tanjong Tokong in the northeast part of the island. On this important day, the Chinese inhabitants headed to the cemeteries to clean the gravesites and pay their respects to their deceased ancestors. Mount Erskine was named after John James Erskine, a member of the town council of Georgetown around 1810. Much of it was taken up by the Chinese cemetery dating back to the early nineteenth century, shared by several ethnic Chinese groups: Cantonese, Teochew, and Hokkien; the last group being the biggest one on the Penang Island.

Ah Yee had been busy buying and preparing baskets of cooked food, freshly decorated oranges, paper money, incense, and joss sticks to bring to Mount Erskine to honor our forebears. She dressed the young ones in their best while the older siblings washed and took care of themselves.

My father realized he had miscalculated and he could not pack all of us onto the bicycles. So he hired a *beca* and went ahead himself. Settling on the padded seats of the human-powered pedicab with Kuan May and me on Meng Kee and Fong's laps, our rickshaw puller lifted up the yoke to his waist, tossing us back into the seats. It was mid-morning under the burning tropical sun. He pulled us along the steamy asphalt road. Wiry and old, tanned and thin with wispy white hair and a goatee, he wore a pointed straw hat, a partially unbuttoned black shirt flapping in the wind, revealing his rib cage, and a pair of loose black trousers with a well-worn towel hanging from his waistband. On his feet he wore a pair of tire sandals, *flip-flop flip-flop*, he ran steadily. Periodically he took out his towel to wipe the glistening sweat off his face and neck. Our ride was smooth but I felt sorry for him, an old man, toiling so hard in the searing heat. After what seemed like ages winding along several roads, he finally arrived at the edge of the cemetery. My father waited for us by Gottlieb Road wearing his pith helmet, looking dapper in his white shirt and khaki shorts. Without warning, the rickshaw man put down his yoke and we lurched forward. We hopped out as my father paid him.

We climbed up the slope of Mount Erskine, covered with hundreds of graves among blades of tall, dry *lalang* grass rustling in the breeze. In the distance wisps of smoke rose from the burning of fake paper money as offerings for the departed. We kept on climbing up a series of old stone steps hidden by the overgrown *lalang* until we finally found the rest of the family clustering around some graves. How my father managed to find the ancestral tombs was a mystery; there were no signs to help him locate them.

Ah Wee wielded his machete, cutting the *lalang* on the gravesite, and applied fresh red paint to the characters carved into the stone slabs. Ah Yee set up tin cans with burning joss sticks in front of each tombstone and offered provisions to our ancestors. Nearby, a group of mourners knelt in front of the tombstones of their loved ones, beating their bosoms, wailing. We sat on the grass under the shade of the umbrellas to have our picnic. Despite the heat and humidity, we enjoyed the outing. In the late afternoon when we were ready to go back to River Road, the rickshaw man was already waiting at the bottom of the cemetery.

This would be the only *Qingming* we went to as a family. It was a big and elaborate arrangement and placed a hefty financial burden on my father. As children, we enjoyed this outing as a family picnic, but for my father, it meant paying respect to his ancestors. The trek up Mount Erskine did not bring me any closer to my ancestors; I had never met them. My father believed that when he passed, to have a good life in the afterworld, he would have to depend on his male children to leave him offerings at the altar or the gravesite. I, as a girl, would not be able to fulfill his wish. But I did not share in either of his beliefs. In later years when we moved away, Mount Erskine became too far for us to visit. Ah Wee and my father went on their own to clear the graves of *lalang,* apply fresh red paint, and leave offerings.

My father was out very early in the morning and back by sundown. One weekend, Ah Yee dressed us up in our best and we trooped to the City Council Club at the *padang* or the big field. All the civil servants and their families including the Tamil laborers were invited for lunch, games, and activities. The higher officials, the Eurasians, and my father sat on a raised platform, although he was delegated to a corner, he claimed a stake up there. We ate a delicious lunch but the best was ice cream in a paper cup which we ate with a wooden stick, courtesy of the Cold Storage Creameries. It was the first time I tasted ice cream, so soft and creamy. Years later I had my first ice cream sundae; it surpassed my experience of that first taste of ice cream.

If I thought ice cream was a treat that only the rich could afford, the ice cream sundae was fit for a king. There were talent shows by the children and all participants were given a prize, but we were too shy to go to the microphone. The mandatory retirement age was fifty-five years for all government servants. When I was five, my father reached his retirement age. Ah Yee, dressed in her beautiful lacey *nyonya baju kebaya, sarong,* and her green and pink beaded shoes, went with him to his retirement party. They were wined and dined in a restaurant. Late that night they came home with my father inebriated, flashing a gold watch on his wrist. I was too young to understand what retirement meant. Soon we learned that because he no longer worked for the government, he had to vacate the only home we knew. We had to move and we did not know then our new home was to be so far away we would not be seeing our friends in River Road again.

Throughout the first five years of my childhood, we did not lack food or shelter. It was filled with adventures of our own making, no fancy toys or posh conveyance to go *makan angin* like the Eurasians. The gnawing issue of race and color raised its ugly and insidious head in our innocent subconscious minds: our Cantonese neighbors who imagined themselves to be at a higher social status looked down on us and we, in turn, dissociated ourselves from the Tamil Indians who were of darker skin color. Although we did not know it then, we would be headed into a period of our lives where Ah Yee and my father would struggle to keep body and soul together, dropping us into the lower stratum of society.

On the day of the move, my father's Tamil friends came to help with the heavy furniture, loading them onto the government lorry. Our wrought iron beds were dismantled. The house echoed with emptiness. Meng Ling frantically made her mother promise to bring her to visit us. There was no chance of that happening. By the time we moved, Ah Yee no longer sent me to Ahmadkan's house. River Road left me with many fond memories, but I was ready to go beyond its boundaries, to explore a new place, make new friends, and have new adventures. Ah Yee sat in the front seat of the lorry with baby Wan while the rest of us stood in the back with the Tamils and our belongings, waving to Meng Ling as the lorry drove over the grassy field that had been my playground for the first five years of my life.

The lorry rolled onto the tarmac road where Kuan May and I had tricked the children from the Tamil school. It passed the thick forest where Kuan May found her mother of all spiders; Ahmadkan's house; the Eurasians' mansions surrounded by the ixora hedges; and then beyond the bridge that bordered our childhood world, leaving our home at River Road for good.

Part II
Living from
hand to mouth

8

The Malay house in the fruit orchard

The lorry lumbered on for what seemed a long while. The scenery changed from residential areas to busy dusty city streets before reaching acres upon acres of green fields and trees, leaving Georgetown and moving inland into Ayer Itam, Black Water. Penang Hill loomed ahead, closer than ever. The hot, unforgiving sun burned off the morning mists shrouding the hill, leaving wispy strands weaving in the forests and the rocky ledges. The lorry chugged along narrow dirt roads where torrential rainwater had cut deep grooves into the soft red earth, some big enough to swallow an entire tire. Leaving the red-earthed road, it creaked and groaned as it rolled and lumbered over a field covered with shrubs and lurched to a stop next to an orchard with many rambutan trees and a traditional Malay wooden thatched-roofed house on stilts. We had arrived at Rifle Range where soldiers came to practice target shooting on a firing range, next to a Chinese farm at the bottom of Tiger Hill. We jumped off the lorry.

Our house was set at a higher level than the rest of the orchard. During the monsoon season, torrential rain quickly collected on the ground and tremendous runoffs came rushing down to the orchard. It was the bottom house of a row of houses built on a slope; setting it on a higher level prevented the floodwater from gathering around and under it.

My father had the movers place our two tall wardrobes in the big hall, dividing it into two sections, setting their wrought iron bed in a corner, affording them some semblance of privacy. The other wrought iron bed was never set up; there was no room for it. We slept on the floor. My father set up a cot in a corner, this could be folded during the day, using it as his bed if the wrought iron bed became too crowded or hot for him.

Ah Wee slept outside the big hall in a room with seven windows, where our family altar also sat. At night he locked the door with two logs of wood which slipped into slots made for that purpose. Right next to the door, he strategically placed several machetes along the wall in case there was a break-in.

Three gnarled cashew trees guarded the front entrance of the orchard. Rambutan, coconut, durian, jackfruit, mangosteen, and chempedak grew, along with a row of pineapple bushes bearing their spiny leaves. A bamboo grove served as a back border separating the orchard from a slope leading to a big field filled with random dirt paths created by the wandering cows of the Tamil Indian shepherds. Next to the bamboo grove was a dry stream bed, which only filled with water when it rained. Ah Wee placed two planks across it as a footbridge.

A deep well sat fifty feet from the house. Light reflected off the beady eyes of several families of toads living in the holes between the moss-coated bricks. Peering over the edge, I could see my dark reflection shimmer in the water. There was a rope and bucket system to get water from the well. Ten feet away was the bathhouse made of woven coconut fronds and a cement container for water. Our new home had no running water.

In a far-away corner of the orchard was the outhouse with a bucket for waste, but there was no light. And there was no night soil man. Somehow it fell onto Meng Kee's shoulders to empty the waste bucket when it was full, digging a deep hole to bury the excrement.

Ah Yee remained strangely quiet, keeping her thoughts to herself. Thye was not so discreet, she let her tears fall freely down her cheeks as she stared with disbelief at the down-graded living conditions. We now lived in the boondocks; she would be too ashamed to ask any of her boyfriends to come and visit.

The rainy season came, rainwater dripped through the thatched roof. Ah Yee screamed at us to fetch whatever buckets, pots, and pans we could find in the kitchen and place them below the leaks. Some containers were too shallow and the rainwater jumped out of them as soon as it hit. I lay still on the floor under a thin blanket, bits of rain splashing on my face. The cacophony of raindrops hitting the containers kept up all night long. Ah Yee, Thye, and Meng Kee got up several times during the night to empty the buckets and wipe the floor. Thankfully our sleeping quarters were mostly dry. We learned the drill when the rain came; we brought out the collection of rain-catching containers. We huddled in spots free from the raindrops to do our homework.

Like our River Road neighborhood, there was a mix of races living in clusters, in their own homes, unintegrated. The exceptions were a Malay family who owned a car—they lived in the last house of the two rows of stucco terraced houses among the Chinese. And the occupants of the row of Malay houses where we lived, with a mix of Malay, Chinese, and Indian races. I remembered the father of the Malay family fondly because, on most Fridays, he set up a screen and projector in his front porch and sent word to the children to come for an evening movie of the Looney Tunes with characters such as Bugs Bunny, Roadrunner, Porky Pig, and Daffy Duck. For a blissful hour, I watched the cartoons spring to life and felt a sad pang in my heart when the iconic cursive *The End* graced the screen.

All the stucco houses had postage-sized gardens in front and back, with the exception of those at the ends which had bigger yards on the sides. A red-earth dirt road ran between these rows of houses, leading to a bridge, and then wound uphill to a field. The other end ran past the front of our house, to another block of stucco houses all occupied by the Chinese. A town green stood in the center. There was a sundry shop of dry goods and snacks; the owner was a hard-working Chinese man, hatching chickens in an incubator, raising them in his side yard. He owned a black Ford, the only other car in this community. Outside this cluster of the Chinese community, the dirt road led to a Malay *kampong* or village and the cowsheds belonging to several Tamil Indian families.

At the back of our house was a different scene altogether, an undeveloped and untouched wide-open grassy field dotted with small shrubs and bushes, stretching out for a distance to the foot of Tiger Hill with terraced vegetable farms and the firing range. When the earth was dug to make the range, two large pits were created; these filled with water during the rainy season. These ponds were teeming with life, especially frog eggs encased in their slimy jelly. We collected these and put them in jars and watched them go through their life cycle.

An array of wildflowers grew in the field, visited by many species of butterflies. Although Boon lost the muddy river for his foray, he had all these to explore, including a clear, bubbly stream teaming with tiny minnows, multi-colored polka dots adorning their scales. He filled a tiny aquarium with them along with some weeds. But after a few days, they died from lack of oxygen in the water.

Beyond the range stretched a Chinese cemetery filled with tombs and mausoleums, each according to the wealth of the deceased. Warned to be respectful of the dead and the spirits, we did not climb up the tombstones unless it was the only way to get around. Several cashew trees, like the yew trees, associated with the dead, grew there. Their fruit tasted bitter. Ah Yee held a morbid belief that this was because they absorbed the juices of the dead bodies. We instead ate the fruit of the cashew trees growing in front of our house but threw away the nuts. The juice left permanent gray stains on the front of our clothes.

Far away beyond the graves, we discovered an abandoned pool, deep in the shade of dense tall trees, only two of the walls remaining. The floor was already long gone; the water became muddy as soon as we jumped into the pool. On a hot day after our exploration, the cool water was welcome for a refreshing dip. I stayed in the shallow end along with several tiny frogs while my older siblings learned to swim at the deep end.

Rifle Range had a shooting range for the British Army and, after independence, the Malayan military and the police. In the morning, truckloads of soldiers arrived, bright and early, to train. Right behind the range was terraced farmland on the slopes of Tiger Hill. Thousands of bullet casings were buried in the range. Some hot afternoons, Kuan May and I went there to scour for them, selling them as scrap metal for some pocket money, risking being yelled at by the farmers for trespassing.

Behind the bamboo grove of the orchard, dense low bushes grew on a lumpy field, stretching for a hundred meters toward the cow paths where we learned to bike, fly a kite, or spent the evening lying on the ground looking at the moon and stars. The grass there was kept short by the grazing cows and goats. The field continued beyond the cow paths, touching the border of the Chinese cemetery.

Ah Wee attempted to grow groundnuts in the lumpy field, but they failed to thrive. One day, official-looking men carrying maps came to survey the land, coming close to our bamboo grove. They dug and uncovered numerous gruesome pieces of bones: skulls, ribs, vertebrae, femurs, hand and foot bones, and loaded them into gigantic wooden crates. The lumpy ground turned out to have been shallow mass graves from the Pacific War. When the British surrendered to the Japanese on February 15, 1942, the Imperial Japanese Army's Kempeitai, the secret police, carried out the infamous Sook Ching, a systematic purging of overseas Chinese in Singapore and Malaya over a two-week period, rounding up and killing thousands of them. At night, eerie green lights floated over the lumpy field. Ah Wee believed they were emitted from the bones of the dead. The thought of the dead bodies exuding toxic fluids which were then absorbed by the groundnuts turned my stomach.

Relatives of the war victims came to mourn their loved ones, elderly women crying inconsolably. Because these were mass graves, the government did not identify the victims. The crates were transported to the crematorium next to the Chinese cemetery, kept busy emitting plumes of black smoke from its many chimneys. When all the ground was combed through, it was flattened out. The weeds took over as the monsoon rains and tropical sun nourished the land, leaving no trace of the recent disturbance. That place remains in my mind a haunted ground.

After the uncovering of the mass grave, nightmares about wars plagued me. I dreamed that war broke out right over Rifle Range, gunfire flared on the horizon, approaching closer as my family packed up to escape. My constantly pregnant mother had trouble moving quickly, and I feared leaving her behind.

I woke suddenly, unable to go back to sleep.

—

Ah Wee was a young man by the time we moved to Rifle Range. He worked for the City Council Transport Department repairing and maintaining the buses. He had the idea of building a badminton court in the field at the back of the house. Badminton was a favorite national sport. Using a hoe, he cleared the land and built a court with perfectly flat ground complete with borders, markings, poles, and netting. He bought a couple of rackets and shuttlecocks. When we wore out the shuttlecocks, we caught Ah Yee's chickens and pulled out three of the biggest feathers and fashioned one with a few round patches of inner bicycle tubes as the base. There were more than a few grumblings from the tortured chickens

In the evening after dinner, we gathered in the field next to the bamboo grove, enjoying the cool breeze. We made friends with our new neighbors; the boys played *ba-ku-li* or marbles and *gasing* or top spinning while the girls jumped ropes to the rhyme of "Bluebells Cockleshells."

Our closest neighbors were a young Malay couple with two small children. The soft-spoken Rahman bicycled to work every day, and when he came home, he changed into a singlet and a blue-and-white checked cotton *sarong* rolled up at the waist, just like my father, spending his time tending his fruit orchard of rambutans, mangoes, and bananas.

Darkness descended on our world, so close to the Equator, without warning. Growing up in rural Malaya, stories about Malay ghosts abounded. Dusk was when ghosts were said to roam freely, subtly announcing their presence with a slight breeze ruffling our clothes or hair, a rustle of the leaves, or an intoxicating fragrance lingering in the air. Fear and uncertainty crept into my sub-consciousness. The proximity of the enormous Chinese cemetery and the mass grave made the presence of roaming ghosts palpable.

Each banana tree flowers and bears fruits only once, then the trunk has to be carefully chopped down to the ground, allowing the creeping horizontal stem to grow a new tree. Rahman showed Ah Wee how to properly chop down a banana tree to prevent *Hantu Tek-Tek*, a female ghost with pendulous breasts, from rising from the stump. Depicted either as a young and beautiful lady or a withered angry old woman favoring young and attractive men, the ghost forced them to drink her milk and suffocated them with her ample breasts.

In the Malay *kampong*, there were a number of champak trees that grew to a great height with low horizontal branches extending for several feet. Their small delicate gold or orange flowers had a distinctive and over-powering sweet fragrance. According to the Malay folklore, *Pontianak*, the Malay equivalent of a vampire, lurks around these trees. Dressed all in white and wearing a champak flower in her hair, she appears at a quick glance to be very attractive but on closer perusal she has menacing razor-sharp teeth. Emerging after sunset, she seeks men or pregnant women and sucks their blood, ripping the fetus from a pregnant woman's womb and devouring it. I tried not to be near the champak trees at dusk.

Fong was given the task of preparing breakfast for the children during the weekdays. When the wall clock in the hall stopped ticking because someone forgot to wind it, she made me go beyond the bamboo grove, up the slope to look for the time on the clock tower of the reservoir. My feet were wet with dew as I ran up the slope. I saw the green flickering, floating lights in Ah Wee's groundnut patch. My heart almost stopped.

Fong's grin when I came back to the house to report the time confirmed my suspicion that she relished sending me on the errand. If she had to wake at an ungodly hour, her sister should suffer along with her.

—

Kuan May and my younger siblings were prone to fever convulsions. With my father retired, Ah Yee was careful about how she spent money. Buying medicines to lower their temperature was not her priority, and she was not quick to give them sponge baths either. One of my younger sisters woke with a fever and stayed on the floor under her blanket while we prepared for the day. She started convulsing, her eyeballs rolling back into her sockets, her tongue sticking out, and froth gathering at the corners of her mouth. Ah Yee became hysterical.

The girl then vomited and turned blue. Ah Yee wrung her hands, at a loss for what to do. My father was not home. I rushed to Rahman's house, calling for help. Lifting up his *sarong*, he raced up the flight of stairs to the bedroom, picked up the convulsive baby, rolled her to her side, thrust a spoon into her mouth to protect the tongue, and began rubbing on her chest to revive her. When the seizure stopped, he had me retrieve a bowl of water and gently sponged her.

Ah Yee stopped trembling. She blamed our overindulgence in eating jackfruit as the reason for my siblings having more frequent convulsions since we had moved to the fruit orchard.

—

In the house next to Rahman lived a girl who was confined to the house. She sat with her father on the enclosed front porch in her lovely chiffon dress and with her hair in ringlets, just like Alice in Wonderland. Ah Yee let us run free, and we had our adventures. I did not envy her beautiful clothes or hair-do, preferring my freedom to explore and play with my siblings. We picked and ate sweet mulberries, staining our tongues, lips, and hands a deep purple, which this girl in her pretty dress was never free to do.

Next to this house was another Malay family we did not know. They threw a lavish wedding lasting several days. Kuan May and I crouched and gawked from behind the bushes. On the final day of the celebration was the *Majlis bersanding*, the wedding reception, the bride and groom wearing the traditional Malay wedding clothes with the bride in her *baju kurung* and *tulong* and the groom, *baju Melayu, songkok,* and *sampin*, they sat together cross-legged on a raised dais adorned with garlands of orchids, gardenias, and frangipanis. Guests climbed up to the *merinjis* and offered their blessings, throwing *bunga rampai*, perfumed pandan leaves, liquid rice flour, and rose water over the couple. They, in turn, presented their guests with *bunga telur,* eggs decorated with flowers symbolizing fertility. My mouth watered at the array of food.

Beyond the last house of our row of Malay houses were a Malay *kampong* and an Indian community with their mud houses and a few barns for cows and goats. Shortly after we moved to Rifle Range, Kuan May and I wandered into the *kampong*. We heard crying. A Malay boy sat on a stone wailing and in front of him was the *Imam*, an older Malay man wearing a white cap, and a group of young boys sitting on small rocks next to him. He was sharpening a knife and a chicken sat beside him. We did not stay to watch him sacrifice the poor chicken. We had inadvertently encroached on a *berkhatan*, circumcision ceremony, the rite of passage for Muslim boys to adulthood. Later I saw the Malay boys wearing *sarongs*, walking with their legs spread far apart.

In the hot and dry month of January or February, the Tamil community celebrated Thaipusam, a Hindu festival that took place during the full moon in the tenth Tamil month of Thai. It commemorates the birthday of the youngest son Lord Muruga or Lord Subramaniam of Shiva and Parvati. Parvati gave her son a *vel* or lance to help him vanquish the evil demon Soorapadman. It is also a day of thanksgiving and penance for the Hindus, believing their sins can be cleansed on that day. Devotees whose prayers had been answered by Lord Muruga, helping them to avert a calamity, vowed to carry a *kavadi*, an ornate arched canopy, on their shoulders supported by a harness on the waist. For a month prior to the festival, they cleansed their bodies through fasting and abstinence; they meditated and ate a vegetarian diet.

On the eve of Thaipusam, two bulls, richly decorated with painted horns, wearing floral garlands of jasmine and marigold and ornate saddles, pulled the statue of Lord Muruga on a bejeweled silver chariot from the Kovil Veedu Temple to the Nattukkottai Chettiar Temple on the slope of Waterfall Road. The statue was bedecked with gold, diamonds, emeralds, and rubies. Devotees cleansed the route by smashing hundreds of fresh coconuts. On arrival at the Nattukkottai Chettiar Temple, they fulfilled their vows, carrying *kavadi* decorated with flowers, peacock feathers, fruit, colored paper, and tinsel. Numerous metal spikes and hooks from the canopies skewered into their chests and backs, miraculously without any sign of bleeding. While in a trance, they hauled decorated bullock carts by the hooks pierced through the skin on their backs. Some carried pots of milk and practiced the mortification of their flesh by piercing their cheeks, tongues, and foreheads with spikes, skewers, and other metal implements. On the third day of the festival, the procession of Lord Muruga and the devotees carrying *kavadi* wound their way from the Nattukkottai Chettiar Temple in the evening back to the Kovil Veedu Temple, arriving in Little India in Georgetown before dawn.

At the Hindu temple in Ayer Itam, I watched this procession of frenzied devotees dancing and prancing barefoot. Saliva dripped from their mouths as their pierced tongues prevented them from spitting or swallowing. A red-hot coal pit burned at the back of the temple, *orang putih*, or white people, sat in the front row seats. I squeezed my way through the crowd and came close to the fire pit and felt the heat on my face. The fire walker stood at one end of the pit, readying himself to walk across six feet of burning coals. Just when he was about to set his first foot onto the hot coals, the swaying crowd blocked my view. There was a roar. Desperately I looked through the gap between the legs of the spectators but only caught a glimpse of the bare feet of the fire walker flying across the coals, ending his perilous walk in a trough of milk with the sounds of singeing and hissing.

In the temple, a big Indian man with an enormous paunch paid his penance by lying on a bed of nails. Images of deities with six arms, elephant trunk, and snakes coiling around their bodies, images fit for a nightmare, adorned the walls and the pillars. I left the temple with a feeling of unease in my heart.

Once a year, around All Souls' Day, the Chinese opera came to the Cemetery of Batu Gantong near Rifle Range to appease the dead from haunting the place. The stage was set up in an open field close to the crematorium and the cemetery. There were two shows, one in the early afternoon in the heat of the day and another in the cool evening. The afternoon show was a comedy featuring the lesser actors. Because it was the hottest part of the day, attendance was sparse. The older folks were there with their grandchildren, a rare moment to enjoy free entertainment. The evening opera was more serious, tended to be longer, and often lasted past midnight. There was music, singing, martial arts, acrobatics, and operatic acting; virtues such as loyalty, morals, love, patriotism, and faithfulness were often reflected.

At my age, I barely understood the story but enjoyed looking at the heavily and beautifully made-up opera characters. In between scenes, I ran backstage with other children to watch the actors apply their makeup. They first smeared a white foundation on their faces followed by a bright red coloring around the eyes, fading toward the bottom of the cheeks. They painted their lips bright red and their eyebrows black, elongating them beyond their normal length. A scalloped hairline over the forehead with sideburns pointing toward the chin framed the face. After this elaborate makeup, the actors got a facelift by tightening the skin near the temples with ribbons tied at the back of the head, lifting up the corners of the eyes. With the swish of their long sleeves, they shooed us away, making us scream as we ran helter-skelter.

When I grew tired of watching them, I went to the side of the stage to watch the musicians, skinny and dark men always with cigarette butts dangling from the corners of their mouths, long burned ashes hovering dangerously at the tips. Stripped to the waist, they wore only shorts with rolled edges. There were the *yehu, erhu, gaohu, pipa,* drums, and cymbals. Music played a big role in the narration of the opera. A sustaining high pitch sound led us to anticipate something dramatic. A continuous ticking sound signified the appearance of a spirit or a ghost, and this was further dramatized by flashes of light on the stage. Dressed in a white flowing robe, with long black hair draping over its face, the specter jumped on the stage with arms outstretched. This never failed to startle us.

The costumes ranged from simple to elaborate, decorated to the hilt with stones, sequins, metallic thread, and embroidery. The fine ladies dressed more resplendently than the maids and simple folk. Headdresses indicated social status and were decorated according to the class of the characters. Scholars and officials wore less showy hats while the generals had hats decorated with long pheasant feathers which they could swish in a dramatic fashion when expressing anger. On their belts, the generals carried a sheathed sword, and one hand often rested on the hilt as they strutted about the stage. Their makeup emphasized their ferocity with thick bushy raised eyebrows and red faces invariably accompanied by a long beard trailing as far as the waist.

When the opera ended, Kuan May and I took a shortcut through the cemetery to go home, picking our way with care in the dark, walking between the massive mausoleums enclosed with wrought iron fences guarded by fierce-looking warriors or Chinese lions, and concrete graves with headstones and enclosed with a circular mound of earth. Some mounds had flattened or even caved in, making them look even more sinister. In the dark, these graves loomed massive and menacing with their shadows thrown across neighboring mounds.

Rifle Range became our home for a number of years before a developer came and stole our idyllic life from us. It seemed far more complicated, steeped in cultural differences I was just beginning to discover and appreciate. We were the Chinese, the Malays, and the Indians, immigrants from different far-flung corners of the earth, brought together by some stroke of fate, carving out our separate lives according to our own customs, traditions, and religions in our adopted country.

9
The Swindlers

My father had a pension after his retirement. He decided to take it out as a lump sum, having the idea that he would invest it, hoping to make it grow.

He had been in discussion with some businessmen about this possible investment. Two young Chinese men, each carrying a black briefcase, identically dressed in dark suits and ties with hair shiny, thick, and slick with Brylcreem, arrived at our Malay house in their white Buick Anglair. They sat on the front porch talking in whispers as my father leaned forward, cupped his right ear, and listened intently. He gazed at them, just nodded, and asked few questions. Since his retirement, he had always worn his gold watch proudly on his wrist, and the young men were eyeing it. After they left, he sat alone, deep in thought, puffing on his pipe. He did not discuss any of their proposals with Ah Yee or anyone.

"Ah Pa, they just want to cheat you of your money," Fong said.

"What do you know? You're just a girl," he grumbled.

I stood and watched in awe. I did not know what my father was thinking but he sure had many mouths to feed, and at age fifty-five he was already jobless. There was no reliable source of income if the pension was gone in a puff of speculating smoke. And Fong was stepping up to protect us.

A week later the young men came back and took off their shoes at the front steps. This time they seemed to be in a hurry to complete their transaction. Boon and Fong climbed the rambutan tree closest to the front porch. Kuan May and I situated ourselves below the floor and poked their socked feet through the cracks with coconut frond sticks. We suppressed our giggles as we watched them perform little dance steps to avoid being stabbed. They did not let on that we were playing a prank on them. One of the men opened his briefcase and showed my father its contents. Fong caught a glimpse and saw bundles of money, she told us later. My father's eyes opened wide. They made him believe that he was sure to catch a windfall, a ploy they used to entice him to enter into an agreement with them.

They rolled out a piece of paper for him to sign. Fong seemed wise for her young age of eleven and spoke up again. "Don't sign it. They will take your money and you will never see them again."

The men remained unmoved and did not once look at Fong. They pushed the ink pad toward my father. Sitting there with a serious face, he offered his right thumb. One of the young men grabbed it, planted it firmly on the ink pad, and placed his thumbprint on the paper. They waited for the ink to dry, placed the signed paper carefully in the briefcase, closed it, stood up, and shook hands with him, promising to return.

Fong called out, *"Phiàn-lâng."* Swindlers.

Stone-faced, they climbed down the front steps, bent down to put on their shoes, walked down the front garden path, and out of our lives forever.

My father never heard from or saw them again.

"Tiam la!" Keep your mouth shut! Father yelled at Fong.

"It was my business what I did with my money."

"How're you going to feed your family?"

"You're the oldest. You will bring up your brother and sisters. You will take care of us in our old age." He pointed to Ah Yee and himself.

"I didn't ask to be born, and these are not my children. I don't care if you're dead; you're still responsible for them."

He never once laid hands on her. With any of the children, perhaps with the exception of Boon, he would have beaten us to a pulp for saying such harsh things. Somehow, she was able to cross the boundary and push his buttons without incurring his wrath.

The comfortable lives we had enjoyed at River Road eluded us after we moved to the orchard. Barely a year after retirement, my father had lost his entire pension. The gold watch went missing from his wrist; he had pawned it to get money to start a business.

One day, with a great deal of pride, he came home with a vendor food cart powered by a bicycle, intending to sell *ice kachang,* a shaved ice bean dessert, and Penang *rojak,* a spicy fruit salad. An identification card from the health department with his picture hung from his neck. He had become a licensed food vendor.

He stationed his food cart under a huge bamboo grove next to the Chinese cemetery at Rifle Range. The dense bamboo provided ample shade from the hot sun and shelter from a brief tropical rain. The Rifle Range flats were just a stone's throw away and the residents frequented his cart. At the end of a long day, we helped clean up the cart, our reward was the leftovers. We welcomed the extra food.

When business slowed down in the lull of the afternoons, he rode his cart to another location, ringing his bell. It was on one of these trips that his cart tumbled over a hilly road. He was badly bruised and cut, lost his front teeth, but did not break any bones. The wheels of the cart were mangled, forcing him to dish out his hard-earned cash for the repair.

After the accident, Boon and Kuan May helped my father with the food cart after school. Fong, being the first-born, was never expected to help. Some afternoons after I finished my homework, I went to the bamboo grove to help. At sundown Kuan May and I pushed the cart over the steep hill where my father had fallen, heading for home. He had taken the afternoon off to buy supplies and invariably stopped at the toddy shop for a drink.

Tired and exhausted, Kuan May had difficulty concentrating on her homework in the evenings. The daily grind had taken a toll on her marks. My parents did not pay much attention to our progress in school. Fong signed our year-end report cards as Ah Yee could not read or write and my father did not know about their existence.

The cart business brought in barely enough money to clothe and feed the family; we were living a hand-to-mouth existence. Ah Yee waited anxiously each night for my father to hand her the money for the next day's meals. Fortunately, the orchard and the house were all paid for before he lost his pension.

The toll of working on a traveling cart was hard for a man approaching sixty; he sold it and the ice shaver. His next move was to rent a stall in a restaurant that served a variety of hawker food—Malay, Indian, and Chinese cuisine.

The Indian stall in the restaurant sold curried rice, *apong*, *roti telor*, *mee goring*, *mee rebus*, fried noodles, and noodle soup. The Chinese stalls offered *chee cheong fan*, rolls of flat rice noodles doused with shrimp paste, chili sauce, and a sprinkling of sesame seeds, and *wanton mee*, a Cantonese noodle dish. My father decided to sell *char koay teow*—a signature hawker dish of the Hokkiens of Penang, stir-fried flat noodles with seafood, eggs, bean sprouts, chili, and soy sauce, garnished with cockles and shrimp. His second offering was *koay teow th'ng*, flat rice noodles served in a clear soup broth, topped with fish balls, slices of pork, chicken, fried golden brown garlic, and chopped scallions.

At the crack of dawn, he went to the market to pick the best bones for his soup base, and buy noodles, meat, fish, eggs, cockles, shrimp, and vegetables. By 7:30 he was ready to serve his customers. He kept long hours, running the store from morning until midnight. Then he biked home, his exhausted body smelling of grease. He no longer had dinner at home. He aged very quickly.

The stall was open seven days a week. To relieve him, Kuan May, Lian Hua, and I helped him during the weekends. As time went on, he wanted us to also come after school to help until dinnertime. When we arrived in the afternoon, he put Kuan May in charge, took some money from the cash drawer, and left. We spread our schoolbooks on the outdoor table next to the stall under the shade of a tropical almond tree to do our homework during the lull.

Our text and exercise books became greasy; the pages were curled and worn.

By six o'clock in the evening, we packed our books to go home. I looked for him on the road leading to the restaurant. When he did not come, Kuan May let Lian Hua and me leave while she remained to man the stall. We took the longer route past the toddy shop, looking for him, carefully avoiding the towering bamboo grove under the bridge where Kuan May and I had once seen a Malay man, his trousers gathered around his ankles as he looked up at us with a wild expression, rubbing his thing near his hairy parts with urgency. We had hurried by, shielding our eyes with our book bags, feeling dirty.

The toddy house was on the bank of one of the tributaries of Sungai Pinang—a big hall with latticed walls and an outdoor patio with many tables and benches. Standing at the entrance, I peered through the haze of smoke and spotted him sitting with a bunch of rowdy Indian laborers drinking toddy, a drink from the fermented sap of the coconut palm, popular among Southeast Asians and the natives of the central Pacific Islands. We called, "Ah Pa," trying to get his attention through the dense smoke and loud noises. But he did not hear us.

Lian Hua and I picked our way carefully through the crowd of men holding mugs overflowing with the sweet, foamy, foul-smelling drink. A miasma of stale alcohol hung in the air. I tugged at his shirt, reminding him that Kuan May was waiting for him. He turned around, his eyes glazed over, raising his mug, not fully recognizing us. The Indian men swayed in their chairs and asked us to leave our father alone. We quickly retreated. Snuffing out his cigarette, my father finally groaned and heaved his unwilling body from the bench. He nodded his head at the Tamil Indians and exchanged words with them in Tamil; they laughed raucously. He joined in, opening his mouth wide, showing his missing front teeth.

Several timid *sari*-clad Indian women milled around the periphery, arms reaching out with open palms, imploring their husbands to give them what was left of their daily wage. The men drowned their sorrow, celebrated the end of a hard day in the toddy shop, and oftentimes forgot they had a wife and small hungry charges waiting at home. Succumbing to temptation, they were lured into spending all their money on drinks. Sometimes a brave barefoot woman waded through the sea of rowdy drinkers looking for her husband, only to be shouted down by the men.

My father downed his last draft, staggered to his bike, and rode down the road unsteadily in the direction of the stall. I stood in front of the toddy shop with Lian Hua, looking sadly at his lonely and tired retreating figure on the bike, praying he was sober enough to ride safely.

Years later when we moved again, the road in front of our house was repaved. A few barefoot Indian women clad in long, flowing *sari* worked on the road in the intense trop- ical heat, carrying heavy baskets of gravel on their heads. They wiped the sweat off their faces with their *sari*, hardly stopping for a drink of water. These were the same Indian women who could not rely on their husbands to bring home the money they needed to clothe and feed their children.

At the end of an exhausting day, they received their wages with their cupped hands and promptly trooped to our neighbor Ah Fatt's mom-and-pop sundry shop to buy food.

He offered only dry goods; beans, peas, potatoes, pasta, rice, and canned products, more expensive than what they could get in the wet market. Despite their daily wages, they still owed him money. Ah Fatt raised his voice and said in Malay, *"Ta boleh hutang, aku pun mahu hidup juga."* You can't owe me money, I too have to live.

The bigger store down the road refused to do business with them. Tired and worn out, they returned to their squatter homes of corrugated sheets and coconut fronds with no electricity or plumbing. Fetching water from the stream, they cooked over outdoor open fires. Late in the evening, their husbands stumbled in, drunk after their hours of happy toddy time.

Unlike the Indian men, my father handed over enough money for Ah Yee to buy food for the family. Living from hand to mouth meant that he had to work every day. Missing a day of work would mean no food on the table for us. He took over the stall in the evening, often under the influence of alcohol. Business picked up around dinnertime and then slowed down until the cinema next to the restaurant let out its patrons after its late-night shows. Ah Yee lay awake every night waiting for him.

10

Chinese primary school

Kuan May started Kong Ming Chinese Primary School when we moved to the fruit orchard, walking a mile and a half to reach it. Penang Island, being a Straits Settlement, had many missionaries, and over a period of almost two centuries they set up schools: the Catholic convent schools; the Jesuit St. Xavier's Institute; and the Methodist Boys' and Girls' schools. Penang Free School for boys was established in 1816, the oldest school in Southeast Asia. Kong Ming Primary School was set up by the Chinese to preserve their Chinese heritage.

Kuan May loved to play teacher and came home every day teaching me all the subjects she had learned: reading, writing, and arithmetic. One year later when it was my turn to register for school, Ah Yee decided she needed me at home to help care for the little ones; she kept me back and Fong and Kuan May were to homeschool me.

Shortly after independence from the British on August 31 of 1957, the Malayan government made education compulsory for all children through standard six. After a year of homeschooling, Ah Yee heard about this education mandate.

Concerned that she was breaking the law, she took me to Kuan May's school to register. At the principal's office, we met with Mr. Chang, a tall, thin, and very old man whose hair was almost all white and whose face was completely covered with wrinkles. As he listened to her, he shook his head from side to side, a corner of his mouth was drawn down, and he spat sideways into the air and all over me. I turned away and wiped my face with my arm, praying that I would not catch his strange affliction. Later he lit a cigarette, continuing to shake his head and spit while puffing.

His head shaking became more vehement and agitated, and his spitting through his clenched, nicotine-stained teeth filled the air with glistening droplets when he told Ah Yee I was here one year too late and he could do nothing for me. Having failed to have me registered, she pulled me along toward the wet market in Ayer Itam, walking to save on bus fare. I was not sure what she was up to; I did not think she did either. We ran into Mr. Li, a friend of my father's, and she told him her predicament, speaking in my father's dialect of Hakka. He reassured her he would fix the problem; the old principal was a friend of his and he was one of the trustees of the school. With a weight lifted off her shoulders, she went to her favorite hawker to eat fried dough sticks dipped in warm almond milk, and for me she bought an *ang ku kueh,* a red tortoise-shaped glutinous rice flour snack filled with mung bean paste. We sat on low stools enjoying our treats, forgetting for a moment that the government might still be on our case.

Within a week I was admitted to Kong Ming Chinese Primary School. Ah Yee dressed me in Kuan May's old school uniform and delivered me to my class. I was temporarily placed in one of the standard one class rooms in the last seat in a corner. I came unprepared and did not have any books, pencils, or an eraser. A student sitting in front of me kindly loaned me some of his. The teacher assigned classwork which I completed easily, having learned almost everything that was to be learned in standard one. The next day I was sent to another standard one class at the end of the hallway. I was one year older than all my classmates.

One day while we were practicing writing Chinese characters, someone threw a pencil at the blackboard, almost hitting the teacher. Immediately she wheeled around in her chair and stood up. Her desk was on a raised platform and so she towered over us. She wanted the culprit to own up, but no one did. Her eyes cruised around the room; we held our collective breath. Then she slammed her book down and announced if no one came forward, she had to punish the whole class. Again, heads lowered and silence prevailed. I imagined someone in the class must know who did it, but I was amazed no one cooperated. She made us stand up, holding a pencil in our teeth and raising our arms over our heads. As long as no one owned up, she left us to stand in that fashion.

At first, some boys giggled, thinking this was all for fun. She walked around the classroom with her cane, hitting desks, calling for the culprit to show himself. She tapped any downward drifting arms with her cane. It was our last period, and when the dismissal bell rang, she just sat at her desk and continued to read. Droves of students stopped to gawk and laugh at us through the three open French doors flanking each side of our classroom, the last room in the school next to the gate.

Kuan May came to get me to walk home. When I caught sight of her, I felt ashamed and began to cry. My cheeks were wet with tears, but I could not wipe them because my arms were over my head. When the school was empty, our teacher finally let us go. Kuan May lost no time spreading my shame to everyone in the family.

—

Kuan May and I had afternoon school. One day we came a little early and the morning session was still on. A little boy with his shirt partly pulled out of his shorts, squatted in a corner next to the hibiscus hedge outside a classroom, casting furtive and timid glances around him. He was small and thin with sandy hair, the unhealthy, light-brown hair of malnutrition. When the dismissal bell rang, he became alert and looked into the classroom but remained squatting. He fidgeted. Another boy with the same light-brown hair, a bigger version of him, emerged. He took off his shoes and handed them over to the squatting boy. He put on the shoes, which were big for him; his toes peeked out the huge gaping holes in the front of the shoes. The big boy patted his head and walked away barefoot on the sharp gravel walk in the hot mid-day sun.

Soon other boys gathered around the little boy, taunting him and laughing at his shoes, *"Liew, liew, liew."* Shame, shame, shame. He looked wistfully at his brother's retreating figure for protection. I saw this delicate exchange of shoes many times between the two brothers.

Kuan May and I each owned a pair of socks that had to last us through an entire week. They were so worn they had holes in the heels. We were embarrassed when the holes peeked over the back of our shoes. I found myself bending down and discreetly tucking them back in throughout the day. When we entered a home, we took off our shoes and socks together and hid the holes in our socks. To put them on without revealing the holes, we squatted down with our skirts around our feet.

No matter how poor we were, Ah Yee made sure our shoes and socks were always clean and white. These boys' white shoes had turned brown, and they had no socks.. I offered him some of my snacks, but like an ill-treated stray dog, he was too scared to accept. No one had shown him kindness before, and he did not expect any.

One afternoon, the assistant principal came to my class, bent down, and whispered to my teacher. She looked up and asked me to pack up and follow him. He was a pale, tall, thin, and bespectacled man, and he seemed to only speak Mandarin. Unlike the principal, he kept his head straight and still and did not spit. The students in the other classes stared as we walked along the corridor wordlessly to the staff room in the main building, adorned with a huge clock. On top of the façade were three flag poles where the national flag was flanked by those of the State of Penang and the school.

The staff room was an echoing cavernous hall; fans whirred from the fifteen-foot ceiling. French doors lined two sides of the walls, and tall glass cabinets filled the other two, stuffed with books and papers brown with age or big jars of preserved specimens. This end of the hall received the least amount of daylight, and in the dimness, the specimens soaked in formaldehyde looked sinister.

At recess I was drawn to them despite their grotesqueness or precisely because they were so out-of-this-world. I hung around the staff room and waited for the teachers to leave so I could sneak in to gaze at them. There were snakes—ranging from the common grass snakes to pythons—monitors, toads, frogs, lizards, human organs, and most gruesome of all, fetuses at various stages of development.

I followed the assistant principal through the staff room, crowded with chairs and desks piled high with papers and books. There were a few teachers hunched over their desks, light from their desk lamps casting a halo around them. We picked our way between the tall glass cabinets and a row of desks and came to a halt in front of an armchair where I found Kuan May slumped like a rag doll, pale and sweaty. For a brief moment I thought she was dead and I began to cry. The assistant principal never addressed me but spoke to the staff attending to Kuan May.

I grabbed her arm and shook her gently. She opened her eyes, took a look at me, and closed them again. Kuan May had fainted in her class, sliding from her desk to the floor. As the clock ticked along, she became more awake and reached into her skirt pocket to pull out her handkerchief and blow her nose. Like our socks, we had one handkerchief a week, and it was quite used and soiled. The assistant principal snorted a derisive and unkind laugh. I fished mine out of my pocket, still folded neatly, as I tried not to use mine until close to the end of the week, and gave it to her. The ceiling fans whirred sultry air around the room; their droning seemed to get louder, pounding in my ears.

Looking up, I spotted a full-grown baby with a trailing corkscrew cord, its legs drawn towards its belly and its thumb poised for sucking. The expressionless glassy eyes returned my glare. I felt woozy. The inordinately loud dismissal school bell startled me. The assistant principal appeared and impatiently asked Kuan May to stand up. She pushed her limp body against the arms of the chair and struggled to her feet, and then he told me to take her home, not knowing that home was almost two miles away. Kuan May leaned on my seven-year-old self as we slowly shuffled our way out, through the gate, down the gravel path, and crossed the busy road with all the children. The sun would be setting in a couple of hours. A car with the assistant principal at the wheel drove by. He did not stop or look at us.

It took us a long time to get home. All the children heading in the same direction had long since disappeared from the dusty red-earthed road.

I never questioned why the assistant principal did not offer to take us home. At my home, we were lucky if we were clothed and fed, the adults in my life expected the children to take care of themselves. The assistant principal had a son my age. Did he ever worry that Kuan May might faint on the way home with no one to care for her except for a seven-year-old?

—

Once during a heavy downpour, as Kuan May and I made our way home from school, the red dirt road was fast becoming a stream of red mud. To save our shoes and socks, we took them off and put them in our school bags wrapped in plastic. The torrential rain pounded on our waxed paper umbrellas which already had holes and rips in them, created by the cockroaches living in them during the dry season. Rain dripped through the holes onto our uniforms, making us wet and cold.

Without warning a few rowdy boys blocked our way, taunting us. Not wishing to confront them, we tried to skirt around them. They side-stepped and barred our way. Desperately, Kuan May swung her waxed paper umbrella at them, which was no match for their metal-spoked black cloth ones. Her umbrella ripped to shreds, leaving behind the naked bamboo frame. The rain soaked through our uniforms, our hair plastered to our faces, and we shivered in the cold. A bicyclist came by, stopped, and yelled at them. They ran away toward the hills with Kuan May giving chase. When we reached home, Ah Yee was more upset about the ruined umbrellas and our soaked uniforms.

She wrung out our uniforms and hung them on a line in the kitchen over the stove where she was boiling water in her black kettle. She sat us down on stools and covered us with a blanket. She dried our shoes in front of the fire, taking great care not to brush them against the ashes and soot. Dinner was waiting for us, and the dishes were kept safe from the flies under a mesh canopy. Later, she ironed our uniforms.

—

Since Kuan May schooled me on all the subjects of standard one, I breezed through that year, acing every subject. I was bored. We had three English lessons a week. My English teacher, Mrs. Wong, was a tall porcelain-complexioned Chinese woman. She wore a slim black silk *cheongsam* with two side slits two-thirds up her white thighs. Despite riding her bike in the mid-day sun, she kept her skin lily-white by wearing a long-sleeved white protective blouse, and she never seemed to look hot or sweaty. She donned a pair of black-rimmed glasses, matching her short black hair that curled inwards stiffly with no visible stray strands no matter the hour of the day; she wore no make-up and her teeth were bucked. Years later when I met her husband, the Chinese pastor at church, he lay down strict dress codes for the ladies. I remembered his wife riding her bike with the front and back flaps of her *cheongsam* flying in the breeze, revealing her alabaster thighs enticingly to the world. Had her husband been aware of it? Shouldn't he have driven her to work in his polished black Ford to protect her modesty?

Despite her austere appearance, Mrs. Wong created a pleasant learning environment for us. Our English reader was a big picture book. We chanted after her, "I am a boy. I am a girl. This is my father. This is my mother." She taught us the alphabet, and we practiced writing in lower and upper cases and later in cursive.

After *merdeka* or independence from the British, we had two Malay lessons a week. The Malayan government made Malay the national language, hoping to eventually replace the English language as the medium of instruction. Our Malay teacher, *Encik* Yusof, a Malay man with a pear-shaped body and a head shaped like a pineapple, had a large nose, heavy jowls, and a meaty double chin covered with day-old whiskers. He wore a pair of gold-rimmed, tinted glasses and a white shirt with sleeves rolled up to his elbows, unbuttoned and tieless. His protruding belly hung over his belt, which struggled to hold up his pair of navy-blue trousers. We nicknamed him buffalo.

The Malay subject was so new there were no textbooks assigned to us. I was not sure whether *Encik* Yusof followed a set curriculum. From the very beginning, he expounded in no uncertain terms that we had better learn the Malay language well, drilling into our heads we were mere visitors in Malaya, and in order to remain there, we were to master "his language." The whole class was of Chinese descent. Unlike my nurturing English teacher, *Encik* Yusof created a hostile and unsafe learning environment for the class. He terrorized us; under his tutelage we did not learn a great deal of Malay. When we were slow to repeat after him, he called us a herd of *babi bodoh*, or stupid pigs. Muslims considered pigs unclean, and since as Chinese we had pork in our diet, we were somehow dirty in his view. Mean and vindictive, he made us repeat after him in Malay we were *babi kotor*, or dirty pigs.

Mrs. Yeoh, our art teacher, wore pink lipstick and her fair and pleasant-looking face was framed by black hair rich with large curls cascading down to her shoulders. Our art supplies, stored in the tall cupboard at the back of the class, were limited to boxes of plasticine, glass jars for water, palettes that looked like muffin baking pans, three powders in primary colors, brushes with thick bristles, and thin paper that quickly got soaked through when we applied colors. We drew the usual things: houses, coconut trees, stick figures, gigantic birds, flowers as tall as the houses, and always a round, orange, happy-looking sun. We could not paint anything refined or dainty with the large brushes. She did not instruct us on the art of mixing colors, and by trial and error, we mixed blue with yellow to get green and red with blue to get purple. Because the spaces in the palettes were limited, soon all the colors were blended together. Our pictures turned into a muddy mess.

Mrs. Yeoh sat at her desk filing her bright red fingernails, and when she tired of that she bestirred herself and walked around us, sprawled on the floor, her high heels clicking on the cement floor. Occasionally she picked up a painting, taking great care not to dirty her hands.

My classmates completed their paintings and left them out to dry in the sun, holding the flimsy paper down with pebbles. We ran to the big by the cafeteria to clean up. Mrs. Yeoh pinned our dry artwork on the bulletin board at the back of the class.

"Stop shaking your legs. It's not lady-like," she said to me. I was unaware I had been doing it. I froze any movement of my legs, realizing this unconscious habit came from bouncing the baby up and down on my lap. By standard two, all my older siblings had morning school. I alone had afternoon school, and I took care of the younger ones while Ah Yee was busy with her chores. If I was not rocking a baby on my lap, I held her on my hip with one arm and a book in the other hand, reading while the rest followed me around the orchard as though I was the mother hen.

When I reached standard three, the students were placed in classes A through E according to the marks they achieved at the end of standard two. I was placed in class A. I remembered thinking that year after year the same teachers were assigned to the same classes. It must be very unfair for a teacher to always teach the worst class—the students in the D and E classes were the least attentive and most disruptive. Often, we heard loud noises and saw paper airplanes flying out of the classrooms. The constantly spitting, crooked-mouthed principal paraded the halls regularly, wielding his long cane.

Our tall and lean class teacher, Mr. Lim, taught us Chinese and Arithmetic. A happy-go-lucky man, always wearing a wide grin on his face, he made learning fun. And after we finished our lessons, he played his number game with us. Huge charts of numbers hung all over the walls and above the blackboards. He made us first think of a number as a class, then he asked a number of questions and through some mysterious process, he quickly and effortlessly guessed our number, laughing with glee like a little boy when he got the answer, and he never failed to get it right.

Encik Yusof was also our Malay teacher in standard three. In fact, he was the only Malay teacher for the whole school in the afternoon session. It was again a reign of terror. Reiterating that we had better learn our Malay if we were to live in Malaya, his country, he made sure we all understood we were second-class citizens.

By standard three, we each had our own desk and chair. Seating in the class was arranged by height. Being the shortest person, I sat in the first seat in the first row. Feeling extremely conspicuous, I was afraid *Encik* Yusof would pick on me, but he never did. Once a tall boy sitting at the back of the class snickered. *Encik* Yusof threw the blackboard eraser at him with such force, it hit the back wall with a sickening thud, leaving a rectangular chalk mark on the wall and a cloud of dust. Some brave boys aimed elastic bands at his rotund body when he was writing on the blackboard with his back turned. Fortunately, nothing hit him and he never noticed.

One morning *Encik* Yusof waddled in and we all stood up to greet him. Without a word, he slumped down on the chair, pulled out a newspaper from his back pocket, unfolded it noisily, and began to read. Within five minutes, he jumped up, put his face close to his chair, and took a long sniff. Livid, he demanded to know who had rubbed garlic on his chair. The silence was deafening. I remembered the incident in standard one when the whole class had been punished.

The boy sitting right in front of him was fidgeting and looking guilty. *Encik* Yusof pounced on him and asked him whether he was the one who had done it. The boy denied he had anything to do with it. Unconvinced, *Encik* Yusof continued to badger him. Then to our horror, he placed his beefy hands around the boy's neck, picked him up, and set him on his desk. The boy turned bright red. *Encik* Yusof wagged his finger in his face, insisting he had been the one responsible for the prank.

Just when we thought things could not get any worse, he snatched up the boy's chair, smashing it down on him. The boy's head went right through the frame, sending splinters flying. He was stunned but did not cry. *Encik* Yusof yanked him from the desk and set his feet on the floor, marched him out of the class, and paraded him along the corridor of the school, choosing the longest route to the principal's office, with him still wearing the broken chair on his neck. Wild with a combination of excitement and trepidation, we rushed out and watched from the second floor of the school building.

Encik Yusof was never reprimanded for the cruelty he inflicted on the boy. The principal trotted to our class and gave us a lecture, shaking his head sideways wildly. His spit glistened in the air while demure *Encik* Yusof stood aside, arms behind him, gloating. For the rest of the year, he continued to enjoy the license to inflict physical and mental anguish on us.

At the end of standard three, I was again the first student in the class. Mr. Lim told me I was to skip standard four so I could be in the same standard as my age group. He was sure I could handle the work. And so, I went straight on to standard five, just one year behind Kuan May. During the school holiday, I tried to catch up by reading the history textbook for standard four; it was all about Malaya during the colonial period. Somehow, I felt cheated of learning that part of Malayan history.

My standard five English teacher, Mr. Ong, grilled us on spelling and dictation right out of the Oxford English Reader. I aced every single test so much so that once I missed a letter in a word and he gave me a score of a hundred anyway. Praising me for my excellent score in front of the class made me even more anxious about achieving perfection. I lowered my head and my face felt hot, wishing the earth would swallow me up. Gently he placed my book on my desk, ridiculing, deriding, and hurling insults at the boys who could not seem to score above fifty. He flung their exercise books down the aisle. My stomach cringed.

To my classmates' credit they never once gave me a hard time for being his favorite.

One day he held in his hand the last book. The tallest boy in my class, who always flunked his spelling and dictation, was all smiles and puffed up his chest like a peacock. Mr. Ong called on him. He stood up, grinning. Mr. Ong remarked his surprise that this boy was suddenly performing perfectly. Unfortunately for the boy, Mr. Ong had decided to leave out a statement in parenthesis on his copy of the work, but this boy kept that in his dictation. Mr. Ong knew immediately the boy had cheated by copying the dictated portion from the textbook verbatim beforehand. Initially, Mr. Ong played along with the deceit and praised the boy for acing his dictation for the first time. Then he changed his tune and became sarcastic as he flung the book down the aisle all the way to the boy's seat. He said for his cheating, he was to receive a big goose egg. The wide grin was erased from the boy's face, and he turned crimson as he bent over to pick up his book. All year he continued to do poorly in spelling and dictation.

At home, I started to mark the number of days left in the school year and the number of lessons I still had with the English teacher on our big wall calendar with the picture of dragon dance. I wished the year would go by faster.

My history teacher, Mr. Chin, was a middle-aged man with sleek, greasy hair, pockmarks on his face, and a prominent black mole on his chin with a few strands of hair. The Chinese believed that a hairy mole on a man was a sure sign of a womanizer, *goh kee chiew,* five whiskers. He always carried a long and slender cane with frayed tips and kept his fingernail long on one of his pinkies. Chinese men, especially those who imagined themselves to be scholars, often grew a long pinky nail to indicate wealth and status, since it proved they obviously did not have to do any manual labor.

Mr. Chin pulled his pants up higher than his waist. He paced in front of the class as he talked, then wheeled around, pointing his cane at one of us and asking for a date in history or a historical fact. If a student offered him an incorrect answer, he called him or her up to the front. Taking his time fingering the frayed ends of his cane while the student faced the class and waited, he aimed for the calves. The girls' skirts would invariably fly up, and that seemed to be titillating for him. Kuan May said he did it on purpose so he could take a peek at the girls' undies.

Standard six was the year I had to prepare for the entrance examination for secondary schools. Students had to get a grade of B and above in order to continue. Fong did not have to help my father at the stall; she had no trouble acing the examination, received an A, and went on to attend the Chinese Convent Secondary Girls' School. My father rewarded her with a new Raleigh women's bicycle. There was no question she was to attend secondary school, which was not required by law.

Boon continued to be the favorite. When the results of the examination came, he could not find his name on the bulletin board under grades A or B. My father waited with him in the schoolyard along with many anxious parents of other students who were in a similar boat. After what seemed like an eternity, a Methodist brother came out and announced that that year, the standard had been lowered and students with a grade C were able to continue into secondary school. He added that God had been good to them and they should take this to heart and apply themselves diligently to their studies for they had been given a second chance. My father came home with a second-hand bike for Boon. We all thought that was fair given that he only gotten a C.

All year long during standard six, my teacher grilled us with quizzes and tests in history, geography, Chinese, and arithmetic. I decided that if I passed, I would go to an all-English secondary school just like Kuan May. I had the advantage of her previous pop quiz questions as she and I had the same teacher. She received a B and I, an A. Neither one of us was given a bike although we remained hopeful for a long while, waiting for my father at the end of every day.

A new English secondary school had just opened up in Jelutong about three miles from our home. Kuan May and I were sent to this brand new school to fill the classrooms. The teachers were not seasoned; teachers and students alike were thrown together in an experimental milieu of the education department post-independence. Whereas Fong and Boon went to schools established years before by the Convent Catholic nuns and the Methodists under the British system, I would be going to a school set up by the young Malayan government.

During the colonial period, the Oxford readers were the main staple. Malayan school children read about English families, their way of life and customs, and nothing about the true make-up of Malaya. The government planned to transform the educational system to suit the culture and customs of the multi-racial country, as a sort of national pride, cutting our ties from colonialism.

Compulsory education came at the right time and saved me and my siblings from the danger of dropping out of school early. I narrowly escaped illiteracy because of the government's mandatory requirement of attendance in primary school, and it saved me from a life of domesticity.

Although when my mother first mentioned that she would keep me at home to help her in the house, I rejoiced at being free from a regimented form of schooling. I did not realize at the time how fortunate I was to be enrolled in school. There was no doubt that I would be kept busy at home, given the mound of tedious chores Ah Yee was burdened with, but after I was introduced to primary school, I would soon learn that there was much more to life than that of domesticity and the drudgery of performing menial tasks.

11

Ah Yee's resourcefulness

While I dreamed about a future free from wants, hunger, monetary worries, and with the freedom to choose and determine my fate, Ah Yee had more immediate problems to overcome: how and where to find a consistent income to feed her growing family.

Wishing to have her own source of money, Ah Yee pinched from the food money and slowly bought a few chickens, ducks, a couple of turkeys, a goose, and a gander. Ah Wee built her a two-tiered coop of heavy wire mesh, the upper tier for the chickens because they could fly, and the lower one for the ducks and geese. In the morning the ducks in the lower tier quacked loudly, jostling eagerly to get out with chicken poop hanging from their feathers. Some roosters and hens refused to get into the coop in the evening no matter how much Ah Yee coaxed, instead, they flew up the rambutan tree next to it, dug their heads deep into their wings, and slept perching on the branches. When it rained they looked miserable; some slept under the house, making round burrows in the dirt.

Ah Yee hoped her feathered children would be as productive as her in the department of making babies. The turkeys grew quickly, filling up with silky feathers. The tom flapped his angry-looking red wattle and guarded his partner jealously; no one could get close to her without rousing him to grunt and open his tail feathers, and wings, circling protectively around her. Getting beyond the invisible boundary caused him to charge and peck accompanied by loud gobbling.

Alas for the goose, always sickly, she did not live long, leaving the gander without a mate. By default, the gander became the watchdog for Ah Yee's feathered brood, warning us with his loud and furious honks whenever a stranger cut across the orchard, coming too close to the coop. I was afraid of him because he once took a full bite of my thigh and twisted it in his bill. The resulting bruise plagued me for weeks. He had respect for Ah Yee, though; he learned not to bite the hand that fed him.

Ah Yee fed her fowls twice a day, in the morning right after they were being released from their coop and in the evening just before they settled down. All day long they foraged for themselves. The soil in the plantation was fertile and full of many fat earthworms. In the evening the fowls seemed to know their feeding time and gathered around the backstairs of the kitchen. She cooed, "Kuku, kuku," imitating the noise made by the chickens (*kuku* means chicken in Malay) they responded with an enthusiastic chorus of kuku. The ducks usually wandered far afield. To them she called at the top of her voice, "Lililili."

From far away, the ducks answered back, flapping their wings, "Quack, quack, quack." The male ducks could only answer in their hoarse, husky voices, "Ha, ha, ha." They waddled home and ate from a long trough. But the gander had a big bowl all to himself. Ah Yee spoiled him.

The first mother hen Ah Yee received as a present from a friend quickly became Kuan May's pet. She named her Ah Kam, meaning gold in Cantonese; she was golden brown. Ah Kam let Kuan May hold her for long stretches of time without complaint.

Every morning Ah Yee poked under Ah Kam to retrieve her eggs; she cackled and grumbled. When Ah Yee sent me to collect the eggs and there were none, I poked my pinky into Ah Kam's anus. She protested with a loud cackle, gave me an offended and angry look, and tried to peck me. I felt the round, smooth surface of an egg and knew she had not laid it yet.

Ah Yee examined the eggs against the sun to look for a spot that indicated they were fertilized. The unfertilized eggs were eaten or sold, but she kept the fertilized ones in a warm can until she collected a dozen of them and put them under Ah Kam for her to hatch. It seemed second nature for her, and she quickly puffed out her feathers to surround all the eggs and only left them briefly to get food and water. She would sit carefully over the eggs, coaxing the stray ones with her beak and pushing them under her wings. We put our fingers underneath her wings and felt the warmth of her feathers. She never pecked us for disturbing her.

A few weeks later her chicks began to hatch, pecking their way out of the eggs, a very slow and tedious process. Once out of the shells, they were wet, slimy, and stumbled about, but soon their yellow feathers became fluffy and they began to chirp. Ah Kam continued to sit on those that took longer to hatch. Ah Yee examined them. Those that had gone bad, she smashed against a rock. There followed a tremendous explosion emitting a stinky odor; egg white and yoke slime smeared the rock surface, and occasionally a dead feathered chick flopped to the ground.

Ten of the twelve eggs hatched. Ah Kam became a proud mother of ten chicks, leading them around the yard, scratching for food. Ah Yee gave them special fine baby chicken feed and fresh water from a bottle. When it was time to rest, they all ran under Ah Kam's wings and slept, occasionally peeking out of the feathers with their sleepy beady eyes.

Ah Kam was productive and hatched several batches of eggs for Ah Yee and became a mother many times over. Sometimes Ah Yee sold her eggs in the market. When Ah Kam grew old, there was talk about having her for dinner. Kuan May was instantly against it and encircled her arms around her, trying to protect her. But Ah Yee was pragmatic, and Ah Kam did eventually end up on the dinner table, although none of the children had any appetite for her. We sat around the table unable to touch our food, mourning her passing. My father glowered at us.

—

One year the chicken flu afflicted the island. Ah Yee's chickens were not spared, and one after another they began to look sick and droopy. Every morning she approached the chicken coop with trepidation and dread, picking up the carcass of the chicken that had succumbed to the flu overnight. It tore at her heart to lose them. She shooed the rest out of the coop, hoping the fresh air would do them good. The sick ones stumbled around, seemingly in a drunken stupor. They refused to eat or drink.

Ah Wee, having worked in the abattoir, advised Ah Yee to kill them before they got too sick to be eaten. So, every day he picked the chicken to be sacrificed and appointed me to be his helper; it was one of the most gruesome tasks. Squatting down on the stone slab in the thatched bathroom, he instructed me to hold the body of the chicken, including its wings and legs so it could not struggle, while he held onto the head, stretched the long neck, plucked it cleaned of feathers, and slit its throat. I averted my face. As the blood spurted and slowly drained from the body, I could feel the chicken's quiver traveling through my arms. It struggled less and less and slowly became limp as the life was drained out of it. He let the body lie on the stone slab as it bled then dumped it in a pot of hot water. Pulling the lifeless body out of the water, he instructed me to help him pluck the feathers till it was clean. Ah Yee cooked the chicken in a soup base sprinkled with cinnamon sticks and garnished with ginger. The aroma usually made my mouth water, but this time it filled me with pain, remorse, and sorrow.

My family enjoyed chicken dinner every night, but I did not relish it. Ah Yee's dream of turning the chickens into cash was dashed. She lost her whole flock before the epidemic of chicken flu died down.

Our bathroom shed did not have a built-in drain for bath water. Fong dug a long winding drain that eventually emptied into a large pit in the orchard. It had to be periodically deepened because of the build-up of sediments. The digging excited the ducklings, the rich earth yielded fat earthworms. Fong was digging one day, and many enthusiastic heads came dangerously close to her sharp hoe. Then it happened, when she put down the hoe into the soft earth, a head stuck in her way and she chopped it off. Horrified, she stopped hoeing. She had the difficult task of confessing to Ah Yee, who yelled at her for being careless. It was a thankless job. Fong gave up finding earthworms for Ah Yee's ducks. And the rest of us were left to do the upkeep.

Ah Yee eventually sold what was left of her flock. She was left with the gander, which behaved as though he was the king of Ah Yee's whole brood, though by now all the fowls had disappeared. While he would never allow us to get close to him, he had become part of our family and so when she announced she had to sell him, we were all upset and argued that he was a tough old bird and no one would buy him. She needed the money and did not listen.

We refused to help her catch the gander. She cornered him in the coop and caught him, but not before she was bitten and scratched. She wrapped him in a towel and strapped him on the rack at the back of her bicycle. The gander pecked at her back as she rode. She stopped and seated him with his back to her so he could not turn around to peck her. As she biked away with her empty basket dangling from one of the handlebars, the basket she hoped to fill with food after the sale, we all prayed that no one would buy him.

Around ten in the morning, Ah Yee came back with the gander, honking triumphantly, still strapped to the back. As predicted no one made an offer because he was too old. We clapped and welcomed him home. Annoyed, Ah Yee asked us point-blank how we planned to fill our bellies that day. She untied him, and he waddled away sideways, looking at her as if offended by the whole ordeal. She consoled herself by saying he would serve as a good watchdog. He was the only fowl we owned that lived a long life and escaped being eaten.

That day Ah Yee had to make a trip to Fat Choo, our neighbor, to borrow money to buy food. She was a kind portly woman with ample bosom threatening to pop out of her *sarong*. Her husband was a businessman and they had a few children of their own. We all traipsed to Fat Choo's house to give Ah Yee moral support. She began with small talk for several minutes before she brought up the subject, promising to repay Fat Choo. This woman understood her predicament and gently pressed a few *ringgit* into her hand.

No matter how hard she tried to make ends meet, slowly and reluctantly Ah Yee began to pawn her gold jewelry. At first, she kidded herself she would be able to get the pieces back, but she never had enough money to retrieve them on time. Then our expandable gold bangles that my father bought for each of the baby girls after their births, when he was still working for the government, also found their way to the pawnshop. When all the jewelry was gone, she had nothing left that was of value to pawn.

Our food budget was one Malaysian *ringgit* and sixty *sen* per day for a household of over ten people (about eighty cents US). One day there was absolutely no money for food. The rice receptacle was empty. Ah Yee checked and rechecked, almost hoping it would fill itself up miraculously. We were faced with the possibility of not eating that day.

Lian Hua found a broken gold chain she had kept in her treasure box. Ah Yee begged her to loan it to her for the pawnshop. Lian Hua stood her ground and refused. The morning wore on and the wet market would be closing. Eventually, Lian Hua handed over the chain, albeit with a great deal of reluctance. Ah Yee went to the pawnshop and we could eat for a few days. Neither Ah Wee nor my father knew about her plight. They came home, and as usual, she gave them the best selection for dinner, never once mentioning what she had had to do to achieve it. A few days later when payday came, Ah Yee retrieved the chain and returned it to Lian Hua, as promised. The rice receptacle was filled to the brim; we felt secure for a few more days. The chain was borrowed twice more to tide us over, and each time she retrieved it faithfully for Lian Hua. In the end, Lian Hua sold it to the pawnshop and kept the money for herself.

—

Secondary school education was not mandatory, and at the beginning of each month, we had to pay school fees. Ah Yee was so tight with money, I had to wrench a promise from her the night before, sitting by her bedside and begging her to give me my school fees. I refused to go to sleep until she finally said, *"Kau la, ke kun na."* Enough, go to sleep. By the end of my first year at Jelutong Secondary School, I was awarded a scholarship as a result of my good grades. I stopped having to badger her.

Because we lived on an island, fish was plentiful. Beef, pork, and chicken were expensive and were reserved for special occasions. We ate fish, tofu, and beans with vegetables. For breakfast, we all shared a loaf of bread delivered on credit by the Indian *roti* or breadman. He pedaled barefoot a long distance, a meat-safe glass cabinet filled with all sorts of baked goods, strapped to the back of his bicycle. He announced his arrival by striking a metal cup with an iron rod, making a welcoming ting-ting-ting sound. Our daily purchase from him was a mere loaf of freshly baked sweet

Bengali roti. When Ah Yee felt particularly generous, she treated us each to a sweet bun or scone. The *roti* man was happy even as his bare feet were thickened and cracked with calluses. He dutifully recorded what Ah Yee purchased in a small, worn account book, and then put his pencil above his ear for safekeeping.

For breakfast, I had one slice of bread and if I was lucky this was either smeared thinly with margarine or condensed milk, luckier still if I had both jam and margarine, especially *kayak* or coconut jam. Oftentimes Ah Yee smeared a very thin coating of jam on all the slices the night before, hid the jar of jam, and I had to be satisfied with that. When there was no jam, I smeared it with margarine, and if she was not looking I sprinkled sugar over it.

On weekends she brewed coffee in her large blackened kettle. She let us each have a cup with sugar and condensed milk, our *kopi susu*, but she drank hers black, *kopi-o*. When she felt particularly rich, she bought a bunch of Ceylon tea leaves and we had this sweetened beverage for a rare treat of afternoon tea, minus the biscuits.

For lunch, to stretch her supply of rice, she cooked porridge. I ate my porridge with half a fish, bean sauce, and a few sprigs of pickled vegetables. Dinner consisted of a large plate of white rice served with a spoonful of vegetables, sauce, and half a fish. We fought over the bottom half of the fish as the top half with the head attached had more bones than meat. Ah Yee always cooked a huge pot of soup: melon, vegetable, egg with mint or onions. She forbade us to drink water before a meal for fear we would become full and could not eat a proper dinner.

Ah Yee gave herself a scant amount of vegetables over a huge pile of white rice, topped with a chicken leg, neck, or fish head, parts that the children refused to eat. Having lost her front teeth during the bike accident, she gnawed at the bones sideways with her remaining teeth, sucking and pulling on the meager strings of meat. She had so many babies at such a furious and fast pace, she was never able to replenish her stores of nutrients and her lack of calcium contributed to her bone loss. She learned from Rahman that the tender young leaves of the cashew trees when garnished with *sambal belachan*, a shrimp paste mixed with chili, were delicious and that would be her meal with white rice if we were short of food. Although she would never admit it, she was hungry all the time, what with the hard work around the house, breastfeeding, and her unborn baby in her womb all competing for calories.

—

At River Road, Ah Yee used coals to cook, but they were expensive. When we moved to Rifle Range, we helped to gather twigs and branches around the fruit orchard and the bushes for firewood, stockpiling them under the house.

Ah Ying, our neighbor, hadn't moved on to secondary school. Cooped up in the house, she was bored and invited me to go with her to the hillside to chop firewood. Knowing how much Ah Yee needed the firewood, I agreed.

Every day after school, I wolfed down my porridge and, armed with Ah Wee's machete, Ah Ying and I hiked through the open field under the glaring sun. Hugging the thin line of trees and bamboo groves for shade, we headed to a small hill a mile from the orchard. Once there, we followed a footpath through the low bushes, the sun directly above us. We picked berries and stuffed them into our mouths, their juice staining our fingers, lips, and tongues a deep purple.

The afternoon was hot and thick with choking, intense humidity. We picked suitable bushes to chop, and our chopping broke the silence, echoing through the hills. Sweat poured from our faces and backs, and the bees buzzed around us. We were thirsty and wandered to a Chinese farm where spring water was piped through hollow bamboo stems into a pool. Cupping our hands under the spout, we drank.

We peeled off bark from the branches and used that as twine to tie the wood. With our bundles of wood balanced precariously on our heads, we wound our way through the bushes back home. Ah Yee's firewood pile grew into an impressive mound. She no longer had to scrounge around for twigs and branches for her cooking.

One day while we were chopping wood, we heard shouting from afar, we could see no one; the bushes obscured our view. As we resumed our chopping, a man yelled in Hokkien, "*Ka ni na.*" Fuck your mother. Ah Ying's already hot face blushed. Picking up our loose bundles and our machetes, we ran down the hill, our hearts pounding. A man appeared at the edge of the bushes.

We stopped going after that. Ah Yee's woodpile dwindled and she resumed buying coals from the sundry store.

—

Lian Hua woke up one day with a swelling on the left side of her face. Ah Yee said she had the mumps, painted the lump with gentian violet, and asked Fong to write the Chinese character for tiger on Lian Hua's swollen cheek. Ah Yee applied the gentian violet every day until the swelling subsided, then she asked Lian Hua to throw away the bottle of dye or bury it in the bamboo grove so the rest of the siblings would not catch the infection.

Kuan May, who homeschooled me, was my closest playmate. Once she came down with a fever, and her face swelled up. Ah Yee found the old bottle of gentian violet high up on the shelf in the kitchen; Lian Hua had not buried it.

Ah Yee went ahead and painted Kuan May's face and Fong wrote the character for tiger on her cheek. I was born in the year of the tiger and wanted very much to have that written on my face as well. I played with Kuan May every day, but I did not come down with the mumps.

When I had a fever, Ah Yee placed her palm on my hot forehead and made me drink a bitter medicine—a brown powder dissolved in warm water—wrapping me in blankets until my fever broke. On the packet of the medicine was a hand with a myriad of symptoms written on all five fingers. It claimed to be capable of relieving them all. One day Fong's fever did not break with this medicine. Ah Yee sent Kuan May and me to catch cockroaches. We winced as she pulled off their legs and wings, ground the bodies to a pulp, and fed them to Fong. The revolting smell would scare any recalcitrant fever away.

Kuan May and I had our own way of breaking our fevers. If we had enough pocket money, we walked a mile through the Malay *kampong* to a *biskut*, biscuit shop, filled with enormous tall glass jars. There was a particular biscuit that we liked—our fever biscuit; the shopkeeper would give us a generous amount of the broken fragments. We raided

Ah Yee's thermos of hot water and added several spoonfuls of sugar. Then we soaked the biscuits until they swelled to three times their original size. The swollen biscuits melted in our mouths, and we drank the hot syrupy water until we broke into a sweat. But when we had no pocket money we reluctantly swallowed the bitter medicine doled out by Ah Yee. Luckily she never resorted to the disgusting cockroaches with us.

Her cure for headaches was either Tiger Balm or eucalyptus oil applied to the forehead and temples. The sickly smell of the Tiger Balm made my headache worse while the cool and burning sensation of the eucalyptus oil gave me temporary relief. I would knot a corner of my handkerchief and douse it with several drops of eucalyptus oil to sniff and inhale all day to clear nasal congestion.

The rainy seasons brought in swarms of mosquitoes thriving on stagnant water where it collected in puddles and empty coconut shells. An Indian man came to our neighborhood to spray DDT, and Ah Wee warned us not to go near him when he was spraying, saying that the spray would burn our lungs and make us grow crooked and deformed. The man remained straight and thin carrying the tank of chemicals on his back.

The mosquitoes covered our bodies with bites, which we scratched until they became infected. Lian Hua and I had weeping skin sores, flies swarmed our wounds, the sores grew bigger and redder, oozing pus. Ah Yee saw us sitting on the stone steps, swatting flies off our wounds, Lian Hua's on her right thigh and mine on my left calf. She sent us to collect leaves off a special medicinal vine and ground them into a poultice. She washed and scrubbed our wounds mercilessly with a brush, using soap and water. We screamed in pain, but the poultice was soothing and cool. She bandaged them with cloth torn from some old clothes and changed them religiously twice a day until our wounds healed and scabbed over. We still bear the scars, but she saved our legs.

A traveling medicine man came to town peddling his wares one evening. Banging a gong, he urged the people to gather after dinner. To entertain the audience, his acrobats performed various acts amidst the clanging of cymbals. During the intermission, he appeared on center stage in his morning coat and top hat, looking like he came right out of Dickens' books. He spouted a rapid-fire sales pitch about his miraculous de-worming medicine, generating huge interest among the mothers in the audience as many children ran around barefoot and most had a protruding belly full of *cha ching*, worms. We ground our teeth during our sleep—to Ah Yee, that was a sure sign of worm infestation.

She dished out the money to buy this awful-tasting medicine. The label on the bottle showed a chubby naked baby wrestling with a ferociously feisty serpent. A couple of spoonfuls of this medicine worked havoc on our tummies, expelling globs of worms the next day.

She made us drink nasty-tasting castor oil when we were constipated, but for the babies, she slipped slivers of soap into their anuses while they screamed. It worked every time. When she had money to spare, she bought cod liver oil and poured it down our throats. The oil stayed stuck there and so did the taste. She claimed it prevented us from developing rickets, a condition that condemned us to a lifetime of bow-leggedness and no one would take us for a wife.

That would have been fine with me. But she never took me seriously when I reminded her I would never marry.

I watched the wonders Ah Yee performed, juggling numerous chores. With her around, I believed there would always be food on the table, even if it was only a meager portion. She performed magic in ways that allayed my fear and anxiety of not having my next meal. Living with her, I had more than a glimpse of the future awaiting me if I should marry. She perpetuated the tradition of favoring boys over girls. The reality of the sexist nature of poverty among the women of Ah Yee's generation, especially those without the benefits of an education, hit me hard.

I needed to find a way to break away from the cycle.

12

The missionaries and their foreign God

My father first heard about Fong and Boon becoming Christians when his friend saw them being baptized in the Indian Ocean at Batu Ferringhi. He sounded the alarm that his children had turned to a foreign god and he might as well abandon hope for an easy life in the netherworld.

A long time ago, seafarers coming as far as the Cape of Good Hope recognized a rocky outcrop on the north coast of Penang as a stopover for a supply of fresh water. This outcrop is now known to the locals as Lover's Isle. The Malays called the seafarers Ferringhi, an Indian term for Europeans or foreigners, and their stopover Batu Ferringhi or Foreigner's Rock. It was ironic that Pastor Adams, the pastor of Peniel Church, picked this place for my siblings' baptism.

My father came home at mid-day, leaving his stall unattended, to confront them about the baptism. What upset him most was that by becoming Christians, they betrayed our ancestors. That would also include him when he died; his spirit would be left to wander aimlessly.

He never laid hands on Fong, and his precious Boon was never ever at risk for a whipping. All he could do was shout at them, his red face turning redder, the blood vessels in his temples threatening to burst. Ah Yee watched helplessly. Wagging his index finger at us, the younger ones, he warned that if he caught us going to church, he would give us a severe thrashing. We were terrified.

"Christians throughout the centuries endured persecutions. God is testing your faith. You have to continue to go to church and believe in Him," Mr. Adams said when he heard about my father's threat.

Who was this Jesus Christ?

The church told us He was the Son of God who came down to Earth and died for our sins. In the book of Genesis, Adam and Eve, the first man and woman made by God disobeyed Him and ate the forbidden fruit, the fruit of the tree of the knowledge of good and evil. God drove them from the Garden of Eden. To save us from our original sins, God sent His only son Jesus Christ, to die for us so we could be saved and be reconciled to God.

My father was a Buddhist, but he worshipped Kuan Yin, the Goddess of Mercy. This often baffled and confused me since females were so unimportant in his eyes, and yet he chose a female Goddess as his primary deity. On days when he played the lottery or when he was to spend the afternoon gambling, he burned extra joss sticks and prayed to her and the ancestors. I never questioned how the beautiful butterflies, fluttering merrily among the wildflowers in the field behind our new house under the glorious tropical sun, appeared on this earth. The existence of God, the Creator, never crossed my mind. Of course, I knew babies came from my parents. What did that have to do with a god?

Besides, Jesus was a foreigner. Was it fitting for an Asian to believe in a foreign god?

Like good new disciples, Fong brought Kuan May and me to church to convert us. It was challenging for us to attend church. We still helped my father in the stall and had to hurry home to wash up and eat dinner. We wore hand-me-downs from the neighbors. Fong was loathe for us to smudge her reputation, appearing poor and wanting.

Pastor Wong was bilingual and often peppered his sermons in the Chinese service with a sprinkling of English words, in his halting, heavily accented English. The church gave me a Chinese Bible which I read avidly, starting from the Book of Genesis, fascinated by the stories of the Old Testament. At church, we delved into the New Testament, reading about the life of Jesus, the disciples, and the magical and enthralling miracles He performed. We had competitive Bible "sword fighting," testing our knowledge of the scriptures. I excelled in this game, blessed with a photographic memory, and could answer with chapter and verse.

Since attending church, I felt a deep sense of betrayal to the Goddess of Mercy. I did not harbor such guilt feelings toward the Kitchen God—he was a tattletale, easily bribable. Our forebears did not mean much to me having never met them. Besides, I did not believe they carried much clout with the Heavenly Emperor. I was just a girl. Did my ancestors really care to listen to me?

Kuan May became the next believer. All the preaching started to convince me that Jesus came to save me from eternal damnation. For me, John 3:16 summed it up: "For God so loved the world, that he gave his only begotten Son, that whosoever believeth in him should not perish, but have eternal life."

With Kuan May publicly announcing her belief in Christ, I felt compelled to declare my belief. At the end of each sermon, Pastor Wong invited the congregation to come forward to accept Christ if they were so moved. My heart pounded in my ears. Fong nudged me. I rose and walked the few steps to the pulpit. There were already a few people standing in front to accept Christ. A warm sensation washed over me, and I felt light and free. Pastor Wong said a short prayer.

That night, I took a giant step away from idol worshiping, abandoning the thousands of years of practice passed down to my father.

I was twelve years old.

Often, my father ran the stall until late at night so we could still attend the evening service. We could not predict when his business was slow, when he would return early and discover we were at church. Wielding a big stick, he sat on the front porch waiting for us. This time he grew tired and went to sleep. We crept under our Malay home, pulled down the sheets Ah Yee left hanging to dry, and used them as blankets, sleeping in the field at the back of the house. When the dew made us cold and wet, we crept back underneath the house and slept on the plank bed till dawn. Our bodies ached from sleeping outside.

Boon removed a few loose floor planks from the room at the back of the kitchen and heaved us through the gap. We took off our shoes, crept in the dark to our sleeping spots. The light suddenly turned on, blinding us.

"Out so late?" Ah Wee said in a loud voice. We froze and waited for my father to wake up, but he was drunk and slept through it. By morning he was so pressed to start his business he had no time to be mad.

He tried another tactic, instructing Ah Yee to cut off our daily allowance. Jelutong Secondary School was three miles away, and without our bus fare, it meant a long walk for Kuan May and me. In the morning, we dared not tempt fate by going into the kitchen to get our breakfast—a single piece of bread. Fong and Boon took us to school on their bicycles, and then they biked to their own schools, all on empty stomachs. In the afternoon, Kuan May and I were not so lucky, we walked home in the tropical heat. Without breakfast or money to buy a snack, we were very hungry. It did not jive with my growth spurt. I was short for my age.

We kept our uniforms and school bags under the house ready for the next day, storing pillows and blankets so we would have bedding to sleep under the house if my father locked the door. Once, as I was drifting off on the plank bed beneath the house, his looming shadow appeared. Boon whispered, "Run!" I jolted from my frozen state and ran as fast as I could, heading to the field beyond the bamboo grove. Being the youngest, I often lagged behind, flinching constantly at the idea of being whacked severely on the back. When all was quiet, we crept back to the house to collect our bedding and resigned ourselves to sleep in the field under the stars. Before sunrise, we got up to change into our uniforms, our stomachs growling.

Not to be defeated, my father's friend told him that as Christians, we would not eat food that had been offered to his gods. Fortunately for us, the fruit season was in full swing, we filled our bellies with rambutans. Kuan May and I continued to help him at the stall where we ate bowls of noodles to satisfy our hunger. Ah Yee could not bear the thought of us going hungry and surreptitiously gave us food that had not been offered to the idols.

My father noticed Lian Hua and and I were absent one evening. The next day he came back in the middle of the day, unannounced. Kuan May had a sixth sense that something was wrong. She told us to hide. Without hesitation, I ran up the hill and hid behind the tree where I often spent time by myself reading, away from the crowded house. I stuck by it until dusk, the commotion from the house did not pique my curiosity. I knew what it was like to be caned by my father. I had experienced it once through no fault of my own. I had been so absorbed with catching *pa pa lang*, dragonflies, by the pond, mesmerized by their finely meshed variegated wings and their controlled flight, like miniature helicopters, I did not hear him call me. In my preoccupation, I failed to notice the lateness of the hour and missed my dinner. He was livid and gave me a beating that seared into my memory. That was why when Kuan May warned us and I did not hesitate.

He beat Lian Hua soundly despite Ah Yee and Ah Wee's pleading. He only stopped when he wrenched a promise from her she would not go to church again. He looked for me, but Kuan May was not about to give me away. I had dinner early that evening, to avoid bumping into him. He must have been spent after the tremendous whipping, drank his bottle of Tiger beer, and went to bed. I escaped unscathed. Lian Hua stopped going to church; she maintained her silence and refused to talk to him. I continued to go to church but with a lot of trepidation. I read my Bible before bedtime and hid it from sight when I was done.

With us as a lost cause for the promise of an easy life in the netherworld, my father made sure he did not lose Ah Wee to the foreign god. He made Ah Wee kneel and pray in front of the altar, burning incense and joss sticks.

Pastor Wong drilled into our heads that it was a sin to wear showy, bright-colored, revealing, tight-fitting clothes. For a young teen, to be asked to wear dull, loose-fitting clothes might have been too much, especially when Twiggy was then the teenage idol. But for me, his dress code was easy to follow; I lacked the cash to spend on lavish, up-to-date clothing anyway.

He warned us about the evils of going to the movies, claiming that kissing and hugging were the works of "the devil." For many years, Kuan May and I abstained from going to the cinema.

In 1965 *The Sound of Music* came to town. Kuan May and I did not see how the devils would have a hand in a family movie. To spend a hot and humid afternoon in an air-conditioned cinema hall promised to be a glorious treat. So, one afternoon, we took the bus with plumes of fumes spewing out of its tail-pipe to the Odeon Cinema in Georgetown. We could not afford to buy sweets, pickled fruits, popcorn, or cold drinks sold in the foyer. Fumbling our way to the front row where the cheap ticket seats were, we sank into them and craned our necks to see the screen. Curls of smoke streamed up from the smokers in the audience to the cone of light hitting the screen. I submerged myself, lost in a far-away world where romance abounded; children lived in beautiful homes with their caring parents, wore lovely clothes, and had plenty of delicious food to eat. For a few hours in the non-sticky air-conditioned cinema, I forgot about our rented home, my second-hand clothes, and my rationed meals. I only woke up from my dream world when the lights came on and the screen displayed "The End."

Kuan May and I followed the crowd to the exit. Outside I squinted at the glaring sun. My hair reeked of smoke; I felt woozy from the heat, the smell of smoke, and an empty stomach. A thought wormed its way in—so much pleasure in so short a time must mean indulging in a movie was not very healthy after all. I did not dwell on the feeling too long. We had to catch a bus home before my father caught us going out to town and gave us a scolding.

Peniel Church, the church where I was first introduced to Christ, dissolved. Boon attended the Assembly of God Church near Georgetown. Kuan May and I found a Baptist Church in the Reservoir Gardens, a new church organized by a group of American Southern Baptists and it attracted many young English-speaking people. We met in a house at the end of a steep road and some evenings we had our service on the lawn under the stars with the crickets chirping. I loved the rousing Baptist songs, livelier than the funereal hymns at the old church.

Mr. Adams left his missionary work and departed for the United States with his wife, Evelyn. I did not know it at the time, but a romantic relationship had blossomed between Fong and Mr. Adams. In the US, he left Evelyn and worked at several odd jobs, including pumping gas, planning to bring Fong over to America. His letters arrived at our home almost daily.

A few years later, Mr. Adams appeared at our front doorstep, wanting to speak to my father. He wished to marry Fong. While Fong fidgeted, my father muttered, "*Lau ang mo qui, boey tua lu eh ah pa.*" Old red-haired devil, old enough to be your father. Mr. Adams was in his forties and Fong was only twenty-one. Should my father have complained or made a fuss about the age difference since he too had robbed the cradle in his marriage to Ah Yee?

Foreigners were unflatteringly nicknamed *"ang mo qui"* or "red-haired devils" in Hokkien, and seen as devious and untrustworthy. My father impressed on Mr. Adams that Fong was his oldest daughter and she might come with a price. Mr. Adams stood his ground and refused to pay for her hand. With misty eyes, my father knew she would leave for a far-away land. I was surprised he did not put up a stink about the interracial nature of the union. Perhaps he had had a little too much to drink that evening.

The day came when we all filed to the Penang Airport to say goodbye. My father had tears in his eyes, but Boon had seen him bawling days before that. The reality of losing his daughter hit him hard—the daughter he had fed by biking through Japanese sentries to buy powdered milk in the black market during the Pacific War—now not knowing when he might see her again.

Before Fong left, she urged me to pursue my education in America and to get a scholarship, promising to help me with my flight. I could not help but wonder if my chance meeting with the missionaries was God working in His mysterious way to pave my way to America.

My father gave up his battle to stop us from attending church, and we continued to do so without much opposition from him. Even so, we made ourselves scarce when he was home so we would not remind him of his failure to prevent us from following a foreign god.

13

My brush with Death

Kuan May and I rose in the early dawn, walked to the bus station in the morning mist, eating our slices of bread thinly smeared with margarine and sprinkled with sugar. I drank water during the mid-morning break while the other students flocked to the canteen to buy their bowls of noodles or curry puffs of peas, potatoes, and meat, to tide them over until school was dismissed at one o'clock. I hid behind the school walls waiting for recess to be over; I did not think the few coins Ah Yee gave me could buy me anything.

It was while I was in form three I began to have trouble reading the words on the blackboard, the sun's rays reflecting off the shiny surface did not help. My math teacher wrote the exam questions on the blackboard, and I misread the numbers, causing my marks to plummet. In desperation, I snatched my father's eyeglasses to help me read the board. He was incensed when he could not find them, but I kept quiet. Where would I have found the money to buy a pair of prescription eyeglasses?

My classmate, Sook Chien, noticed that I leaned close to the blackboard. One day she quietly slipped some money into my hands. I went into Georgetown and bought a pair of eyeglasses, grateful for her generosity and kindness. I set my father's glasses on the table next to his chair before he got home from work.

In form three, our class of ten girls and forty boys had separate physical education classes. My art teacher, who was also my physical education teacher, was pregnant. Even in her non-pregnant state, I could not imagine her being active. Always wearing fashionable dresses, she kept her fingernails long and painted. Her painted toe-nails peeked through her high-heeled open-toed shoes as she sat under the shades of the flame trees with her handbag beside her, donning her sunglasses, supervising us from afar.

For a number of weeks, I felt sluggish, dragging myself to and from school, not wishing to participate in physical education or after-school sports activities. My favorite sport was netball, but even that did not perk me up. My eyes were puffy in the morning despite a good night's sleep. I applied a warm towel over them to decrease the swelling. My calves became swollen and my socks were tight around the ankles. Soon my belly became bloated as well. When I came home from school, instead of doing my homework I went to bed, sleeping the whole afternoon. When dinner time came, I had no appetite.

I asked to be excused from physical education; my teacher told me I was lazy. It was out of character for me to skip a class because I was always hard-working and took pride in never missing any class. While milling with the girls in the locker room after they finished their physical education, one of my classmates told me she noticed my swollen legs and puffy eyes. Turning away from the mirror, she stopped combing her hair and looked at me with her big wide eyes, telling me her brother had died from kidney disease and had the same symptoms. She advised me to see a doctor before it was too late. For the rest of the day, I had trouble concentrating, waiting for the dismissal bell to ring.

At home, I begged Ah Yee to take me to the doctor. I did not want to die. She was busy with the babies, the household work, food shopping, and cooking, the last thing she wanted to do was spend her entire day waiting in the government clinic for a doctor to see me. She continued to do her chores, listening quietly, but did not say a word. It was a Sunday, and Ah Wee was home, he heard my pleading and asked her to take me to the hospital clinic.

That Monday was the birthday of Yang di-Pertuan Agong, the king, and it was a holiday. She sent Kuan May to buy food in the wet market and took me on the bus to the hospital.

Penang General Hospital was a government hospital where we received free health care. It operated as a walk-in clinic and on most days, hundreds of people waited on benches in a large open waiting hall with the ceiling fans whirling. The wait could be an entire day if one arrived late. As it was the king's birthday, the clinic was closed. That day, we were triaged to another section of the hospital and waited for the doctor to show up. There was one other patient in the room, a Tamil Indian man in a wheelchair with his wife standing by him. At first, he moaned, but when the doctor examined his leg, he let out a blood curdling, shrill scream and cried like a baby. I had never seen a man cry before, and he frightened me when he called for his mama.

The doctor asked me about my symptoms and how long I had been feeling ill. He examined me and ordered a urine test. When he saw the results, he turned to Ah Yee, telling her she should have brought me in sooner. He had to keep me in the hospital. I took a peek and saw "+ albumin" in the report. When I was led away to the hospital ward, Ah Yee turned her face away to wipe her eyes; she did not want me to see her cry.

At the women's ward, she helped me change into the hospital top and *sarong*. She had worn *sarong* since she got married, but no matter how much I wiggled and tugged, it wouldn't stay up. The ward was a large hall with two rows of metal beds painted white, each with a small white bedside table. Droning fans dangled from the high ceiling. To one side of the hallway was the communal bathroom. I wished I had Ah Yee's wooden clogs so I did not have to walk with my flip-flops on the wet floor. She helped me climb into the bed, crisp and clean. My first bed in my entire life that I did not have to share with anyone. Worrying about the mountain of work at home, she did not linger, and I was left alone to stay overnight in a strange place. I asked her to bring my books the next time she came to visit as my mid-year examination was approaching and I had to prepare for it.

The hospital food was delicious: rice topped with a pad of what I later learned was butter. I liked the salty taste it added to the rice, and there was always some kind of meat, mutton, fish, or chicken, vegetables, and fruit. I ate well. My appetite returned.

Every morning, the matron and a troop of nurses accompanied the doctor when he examined the patients. They set up a moving screen around each patient, waiting on the doctor like handmaidens. My doctor was a young, pale, bespectacled Chinese man who moved deliberately. I was fourteen years old and had just started my periods; my breasts were just budding and they were tender to touch. I felt ashamed when he squeezed them and hurt me.

The bed rest and treatment with penicillin injected into my buttock seemed to do the trick. I began to put out a tremendous amount of fluid and the swelling in my face, belly, and legs lessened. The nurse checked my urine for spilled protein. I was hardly ever pricked for a blood test, which I was happy about. But every time she came at me with the penicillin needle, I shied away and had to force myself to allow her access to my muscle.

Once she hit a nerve deep in my buttock, causing intense shooting pain down my leg and momentarily paralyzing it. I thought I would never be able to walk again.

The nurses wore starched white cotton uniforms with different colored belts, reflecting their ranks. The first-year students wore white belts, while the second and third year wore green and yellow belts respectively. The blue-belted nurses were the staff nurses. To be promoted beyond that level, to be a matron, the coveted red belt, a nurse had to be single. The matrons were spinsters and almost all of them were older women with thick waists. I knew I would not fancy myself a matron. The nurses were subservient to the doctor and were barked at and bullied by the matron.

My family visited me every day and that made me feel very special. Some of my classmates came and brought get-well notes and gifts. The ward was lit by low-wattage naked light bulbs dangling from the high ceiling, slightly better than the kerosene lamps at home. One night while I was lying on my belly reading my history book about Marco Polo's travels on the silk route, someone bent down, casting a shadow on the pages. Peering over my shoulders, she said, "You'll ruin your eyes reading in this dim light."

I looked up and saw a tall Punjabi woman doctor. She closed my book, petted my head, straightened up, and walked down the hall. I stared at her retreating figure in her white coat over her long flowing Punjabi dress as she disappeared through the double saloon door in the lingering evening light. My own doctor was a chain-smoking mild-mannered Chinese man. This was the first time I had met a woman doctor and the thought stayed with me for a long time after I left the hospital.

I stayed for a total of two weeks. When I was discharged, my doctor wrote some cryptic instructions on a sheet of paper: acute nephritis, rest at home, return in a couple of weeks. I was feeling well and went to school the next day. My history teacher, Mrs. Asha, asked me whether I had any dietary restrictions because of my sickness. My fair-skinned English teacher, Miss Lim, who went to college in England, commented that I had lost weight and I should eat more. That was easier said than done in my house where food was always scarce. I missed the food in the hospital.

The doctor did not explain to me why my kidneys failed. It was later when I went to medical school, I learned that I had contracted post-streptococcal glomerulonephritis, a rare kidney disease as a result of the infected wounds from mosquito bites.

Because of this bout of illness, Ah Yee bore a great deal of guilt and gave me a bigger allowance for school, she added a ten-*sen* coin, but I still did not go to the canteen, instead,

I used it to buy snacks when I returned from school. Not having been in the canteen in years, I felt embarrassed by my meager allowance, not knowing what or how much I could afford.

She took me back to the hospital ward two weeks later to see the doctor. I had another urine test which showed some spilling of protein but much less than before. The doctor said I could now return to school but I told him I had been back and in fact, took my mid-year examinations as well.

"Didn't I tell you to rest at home?" he said. I did not consider going to school work so my interpretation of rest at home did not preclude that.

I aced my mid-year examinations, especially history.

I lost a whopping fourteen pounds, and my period stopped. It was intermittent to begin with when I started menstruating at age thirteen. Thye was the first to have her period and Ah Yee used to beat her up for soiling but failed to explain why she was bleeding. I had learned about the regular monthly bleeding in school before mine even started when the teachers herded all the girls to the auditorium for a movie in which blonde-haired mothers explained to their equally beautiful blonde-haired girls about the periods. Culturally, it was a great leap for me to connect with them. In the end, the company that sponsored this event gave us a polished booklet with the same mother and daughter with pictograms about menstruation and a sample of feminine pads.

It was Kuan May who told me to be prepared with a box of Kotex pads for when I started to bleed. I didn't really believe her, so when I went to the toilet at thirteen and found a dark brown streak in my underwear, I tried to wipe myself over and over, hoping the bleeding would stop. It did not. And so, when my period stopped right after my illness, I was elated and hoped it would stop forever. But a year later, much to my disappointment, it came back like clockwork every twenty-eight days.

It was also Kuan May who took me to a sidewalk vendor to pick up my first training bra. I was embarrassed having to buy mine from a man. Ah Yee was an orphan and her grandmother and aunt had seen no need to teach her the basics. We children were left to learn from each other. Even more burdensome for us, we had to set aside our meager allowances for such expenses.

While I was in the hospital, an elderly woman hanged herself from one of the many cashew trees in front of our house. Rumor had it that she felt ill-used by her children and she became so lonely she ended her life. Kuan May wanted to show me the tree from which she hanged herself but I did not wish to see it. It tore at my gut that she felt so unwanted, so unloved. I felt very blessed to have recovered from my illness.

My brush with death awakened my vigor for life.

14

The end of the school year

In early October, the last of the second round of the monsoon rains came pelting down, accompanied by the strong southeast wind sweeping from northern Australia over the Indian Ocean toward the Malayan peninsula. Thunder and lightning accentuated the threat of the menacing gust as it took with it several *attap* roofs, helpless against its majestic power.

Our final examination took place in early November, weeks before the school year ended. After our exam, there remained ample free time when we no longer had to hit the books. Our class planned a trip to Penang Hill which the locals affectionately hailed Bukit Bendara or Flag Hill. Set at an elevation of 2,823 feet, it was a cool place for the islanders to escape the heat and noise of the city. The hilly and forested area was founded by Captain Francis Light, the founder of Penang Island, during his packhorse track in 1788. Between 1906 and 1923 construction began on the funicular railway at a cost of about 1.5 million Strait dollars to make the hill resort accessible for the populace and easier for the British. In the colonial days, they built many mansions and bungalows as a retreat from the heat and humidity of the valley.

The trip up Penang Hill was the idea of a handful of pupils, who did the planning, with the teachers recruited as chaperones. We rented a bungalow, intending to spend three glorious days, and brought food and spices as there were no stores there. Even though Penang Hill was not far from my house, my siblings and I had never been there. I was excited and anxious because I was not sure whether Ah Yee had the money to let me go.

She did come up with the money. I was elated!

I caught a miniature city council bus right by the restaurant where my father had his stall to the funicular railway station. Most of my classmates lived in Georgetown and their parents drove them. We met at the bottom of the hill. As we ascended, the whole of Georgetown spread below us. My ears popped, the train went through a cool mist, and we reappeared on the other side. Before long, it wound through a tunnel. The funicular railway had a two-section track and passengers changed cars halfway up. The entire journey took half an hour. From the top station, a narrow tarmac road wound under the cool shade of tall trees soaring into the sky. Birds chirped and monkeys swung from branch to branch.

The bungalow sat like a delicate cake on a slope with a vista of Georgetown in the valley. A grand staircase led from the front door to the wide lawn and garden; one could almost picture the British presiding over a magnificent party. Leafless frangipani spread their gnarled branches covered with pink flowers, while the flame of the forest trees flashed their bright red flowers in the brilliant sunlight. Flowerbeds along the walls of the bungalow were filled with succulent purple and white flowers and crinum lilies. The cascades of purple, orange, white, and pink bougainvillea flaunted their beauty. French doors lined the walls, letting in a welcoming cool and refreshing breeze.

The first floor boasted a huge sitting room which could be converted into a ballroom, ornate courtly chandeliers hanging from the high ceiling. Leading off that were the dining room and an enormous kitchen. On both sides of the first floor were two sets of staircases leading to the second floor, opening into spacious bedrooms and bathrooms. The high ceiling enhanced the size of the airy bedrooms with gauzy mosquito nets draping over the beds. French doors opened into an inviting balcony overlooking the valley and grounds. In the evening the lights of the city sparkled like the jewels in the crown of England.

We took long walks, exploring our surroundings, and working up an appetite for delectable sandwiches. We played games in the afternoon, and then in the evening, we all helped to prepare dinner and had a wonderful time eating and laughing in the cool and relaxing mountain air. And there were a few more days of such fun and pleasure.

I slept on a soft bed lined with luxurious cotton sheets for the second time in my life. It was simply heavenly, and yes, there were flush toilets, showers, and tubs.

—

Mr. Tang, our form three geography teacher, was a recent graduate from the University of Malaya. Tall, well-built, and looking debonair, he rode a scooter with his briefcase wedged between his legs. He made us draw topographic maps of the Malayan Peninsula. Lan Fong and I were good at art and we excelled in making beautifully colored maps. Mr. Tang's teaching style was different from most of our teachers who read verbatim from the textbooks, occasionally making some comments. Such classes were long, tedious, and boring. In contrast, he lectured and described to us places we had never been to, challenging and intriguing my imagination.

At the end of the school year, he organized a field trip to the Botanical Gardens. He told us to bring our sketchbooks and paints. He exhibited his own oil paintings at the local galleries. We piled into the school bus on a bright and sunny day with him and our Malay teacher, Mrs. Fatima, as our chaperones.

Mrs. Fatima, as fair as alabaster, was a Chinese woman brought up by a Malay family. The kids were rowdy, but she kept us in line for the journey, telling a tale of a Malay female ghost. *Penanggalan* had dancing entrails dangling from her head, having no abdomen to contain them. Floating in the evening with her bloody jellyfish-like intestines, she preyed on living creatures, thriving on the blood of infants and the unborn. During the day, she lived as a normal woman among humans. At night, she exited her body and hid her headless torso in a tree trunk. After a night of feeding, her intestines would not fit back into her body and she had to soak them in vinegar to shrink them. Being boneless she was able to enter a home by squeezing through the tiniest crack in the woodwork, but a barrier of prickly, thorny branches and brambles around the house would stop her. Her hair-raising ghost tale enraptured me.

We finally left the city and weaved our way through the green countryside. At the parking lot in front of the entrance to the Botanical Gardens monkeys swung from branch to branch. A vast undulating green field with a bubbling brook greeted us. A lone deciduous tree with striking colors of red, orange, yellow, and brown, mixed with patches of green grew next to a small waterfall. I sketched my scene of the deciduous tree and the waterfall, and when I was happy with my composition, I applied watercolor to my drawing. The morning became warmer. Mr. Tang stopped his sketching periodically to check on us. My painting was beginning to take shape. He paused by my side and let me know I had real talent.

We stopped to have lunch and spent the rest of the time exploring the gardens with its many dense and tall trees forming a high and thick canopy. Climbers grew along the slopes of the hills and the tree trunks while garrulous primates frolicked. I finished my painting at home; it was one of the few things from my past that I kept.

—

Our teachers finished grading our final examinations and cash prizes were awarded to the best students and also to the students with the highest marks in individual subjects. Ever since I started at Jelutong Secondary School, I had always been the first girl in my class and for that, I was awarded a cash prize besides winning first prizes in English, geography, history, mathematics, science, and nature studies. Lan Fong and I rivaled each other for the art prize. I felt selfish being the student hoarding all the prizes and walked up to the stage numerous times. I wished I could share them with the other students who worked hard but did not make the top marks.

Before the award ceremony, I received gift certificates to spend at a designated book store in Georgetown. It carried supplies and accessories but no textbooks. I recruited Kuan May's help to spend the money. My treasured finds were Lewis Carroll's books: *Alice in Wonderland* and *Through the Looking Glass*. I bought colored pencils for myself and my siblings, an Oxford pencil box with its contents of protractors and ruler, brushes, a box of watercolor, Indian ink, erasers, pens, pencils, and sketchbooks. I would have loved to buy exercise books, but this bookstore only carried generic ones, not school-specific exercise books. It was difficult to spend all the money I won.

I brought the gifts to the school to be wrapped for the award ceremony. It was a big day and parents were invited. I saw my classmates' parents, all dressed up, beaming with pride at their children's accomplishments, and milling with the teachers. But I did not invite mine. Ah Yee was too busy. I was too afraid to invite my father for fear he might make a scene. So my parents never knew about the ceremony. I did not share with them about the awards I won, feeling they would not understand, they were too wrapped up with earning a living.

The trustees, headmaster, and teachers sat on the stage. The ceremony began with the national anthem followed by a speech by our headmaster. A photographer took a picture of me as a Punjabi trustee handed me my prize. I had on my brown prefect blazer with my long black hair braided into one long braid which was then folded and tied behind my head. The ceremony ended with us singing our school song.

The reception offered an abundance of mouth-watering

colorful kueh: *agar agar, kueh kosui, kueh kaya, nine-layer kueh lapis, kueh talam, kueh nyonya, kueh mingka* ... sweet things that were rarely served at my home because we never had the money to buy them.

When I came home, with a smile on his face Ah Wee quietly handed me a tiny box. I opened it and found a delicate Citizen ladies watch. It was very special to me. I put it to my ear, relishing the metered ticking. When I went to sleep I placed the watch back into its box and, as with the dolls, it spent the night with me. I got up several times during the night, took it out of the box to listen and smell the leather band.

It was a very memorable way to end the school year.

—

The four-week-long holiday started, just when the hot season began. Our English books, written and published in England, would have us believe that most families packed their beach things and went away for a seaside holiday, but that was not to be for the Lai family. School holiday meant we had to spend more time every day, including the weekends, helping out at my father's stall, giving him time to gallivant about town. I did not begrudge him his free time; heavens knew he worked hard enough to eke out a living. On Sundays he let us go back home a little early so we could have a break. We rushed home to get washed to attend the Sunday evening service.

My hair and clothes smelled like grease and smoke from my father's stall despite washing regularly. Christmas came right in the middle of our holiday and as the islanders were mostly Buddhists and Muslims, there was no overt celebration. One evening I was very excited when I saw through the window of a house my first Christmas tree all decorated and lit up. Peniel Church celebrated the birth of Christ but there were sparse Christmas decorations. Pastor Wong warned us against paganism and that the presence of a Christmas tree would invite the specter of Satan to tempt us, so the Christmas celebration was spartan. At Reservoir Gardens Baptist Church, Christmas was celebrated with a fully decorated Christmas tree with lights and trimmings and some church friends gave me small presents. I could not reciprocate since I lacked the means. The church bused us to various parishioners' homes for Christmas caroling, ending up at one home where they put out a huge spread of goodies. By the time I came home, my father was fast asleep.

Then the first of January ushered in a New Year. Big ships docked at the Port of Penang and foreign sailors wearing their smart white sailor suits with blue stripes and caps came to visit Penang Hill. The restaurant where my father had his stall was near the bus stop where passengers boarded a bus to the bottom of the hill to catch the funicular railway. Many stopped for refreshment, always game to try local food.

One day a sailor ordered a big bowl of *kueh teow t'ung*. My father gave him a big helping and inquired in his broken English whether he would like some chili. The sailor nodded emphatically. I watched as the sailor mixed the chili into his soup. Pursing his lips and blowing air through his mouth in quick succession in a desperate attempt to cool his tongue, the sailor signaled the waiter to get him a cold drink. With beads of sweat cropping up on his forehead, he ate most of his noodles and drank the soup. When he was done he asked my father how much he owed him. He charged him one Malaysian *ringgit* while normally it would cost only fifty *sen*. Without hesitation he whipped out a *ringgit* from his wallet. My father carried away the partially empty bowl and chopsticks, trembling with delight. When he passed by me, he muttered, "It's a New Year. He is an *ang mo qui*." A foreigner. From that day on he instructed us to charge all sailors a Malaysian *ringgit* for each bowl or plate of noodles.

That January he made a healthy profit catering to the visiting sailors.

Upon our return, most English teachers were determined to torment us by making us write the usual essay on "What we did on our holiday." I pretended I was like most English kids, my whole family packed up and headed for the seaside to escape the heat.

15

A summer cloud

Ah Wee drew a salary from the City Council Transport Department and helped with the family expenses. Once after school, I visited him in the greasy depot in Georgetown, an inferno in the middle of the day. He showed me around and introduced me to his co-workers—men in grimy khaki overalls. Calendars of blonde girls sitting on hoods or standing next to well-polished shining cars of the sixties, arching their backs, pushing up their chests, wearing very skimpy bikinis and provocative clothes, and showing off their long sexy legs, covered the walls. He came home after work to have his dinner, smelling of engine grease, and his fingernails were forever coated with black soot despite vigorous washing, scrubbing, and bathing. After his bucket bath, he groomed himself, applied a liberal amount of Brylcreem to his profuse jet-black hair, peered at his face in a small sliver of mirror hung in front of his clothes cupboard, and out he went riding his bicycle, to paint the town red.

Meng Kee hired herself out as a live-in domestic help for a Chinese professor. On her days off, she returned home, bringing us apples or oranges from Australia and other special and exotic treats. Accustomed to being alone in a big house, she quickly found the constant badgering of her siblings annoying. No sooner had she returned home, than she wished to go back to her own place. Like Ah Wee, she gave a portion of her earnings to Ah Yee.

One day, my father announced that his older brother would be paying us a visit. This was the first time we learned he had a brother in Kuala Lumpur, the capital of the country, a big, far away city. He asked Ah Yee to be sure to have baby Wan all dressed up.

My uncle was a well-to-do businessman. He came with his wife and an older woman whom my father asked us to address as Ah Paw or grandmother. Dressed in a traditional Chinese black silk *sam foo*, Ah Paw's thin white wispy hair was pulled back in a bun with ebony pins, her face crawling with wrinkles, and she could not be induced to flash a smile or utter a word. Traditionally, many Chinese women remained in mourning after their husbands' death and wore black for the rest of their lives.

Having lost all her teeth, she ate mainly soup; her upper and lower lips pinched tightly on the rim of the bowl, sucking in the content with loud slurps while my aunt held onto the bowl. She spent most of her time sleeping on my father's cot, her pouting mouth partially open and her small bound feet showing through the blanket. Her tiny intricately embroidered shoes sat on the floor. While she slept, I tried them on but I could not fit my feet in them. Her feet were crooked, broken, deformed, and smelly.

My uncle told my father that Ah Paw wished to go back to China, her ancestral homeland, to die. I remembered Ah Sook, the mysterious fourth adopted child who had been sent back to China years before. It seemed to me that bad and old people ended up in China; not a desirable country to be in.

My tall aunt, dressed in a floral *sam foo,* had a broad face, a hoarse voice, kinky hair, and perpetually bulging eyes; eyes like those of a deer caught in the headlights. Her features were coarse, not as refined and dainty as Ah Yee's. Even though her hair had a permanent in the latest style, Ah Yee still surpassed her in beauty.

Ah Yee had long stopped buying herself the scented Yardley Talc, with graceful English women costumed in the style of Jane Austen's characters gracing the tin can, or a cake of pink face powder with a powder puff in a box, its cover showing a woman with permed hair and a face as smooth as silk with cheeks covered in rouge. When she had money to spare, she went through the ritual of smearing her face, and sometimes ours, in the evenings with *bedak sejok,* a smooth paste of a white refined rice powder mixed with water, left it overnight and washed it off the next day—a local spa treatment to keep her face looking soft and silky. But Ah Yee did not need cosmetics to make her beautiful.

My aunt paid very little heed to us but focused all her attention on baby Wan, cuddling her and smooching her soft pink cheeks with her thick wet lips. My uncle and aunt talked to my father in low voices, but they did not include Ah Yee, who was always busy in the kitchen cooking one thing or another for them. My uncle spoke to Fong and Boon in English and ignored the rest of us as though we did not exist. They stayed in a hotel in Georgetown and treated Fong and Boon to lunch, making the rest of us intensely jealous. They had been married for a number of years but had not been blessed with children. Fong said my aunt was barren; I envisioned her womb as dry as a desert, hostile to any kind of life.

The day arrived for my uncle, aunt, and Ah Paw to leave for Kuala Lumpur. That morning, my father had Ah Yee dress baby Wan in her best. We stood under the spreading arms of a rambutan tree by the flower garden to say goodbye. Ah Yee held the baby, picking up her arm to wave at them. At last, my father said to her, *"Hoe yi kiá la."* Give her the baby. Confused, Ah Yee squeezed Wan. My aunt reached over for the baby but Wan twisted her body and clung to Ah Yee's neck. Ah Yee suddenly understood what my father was up to: he was giving the baby away to his brother. Wan started to scream when my father wrenched her away from Ah Yee's grip. Relieved of her baby, she stood under the rambutan tree and began to cry. My aunt held the crying baby, who was still craning for Ah Yee. With her free hand, my aunt handed Ah Yee a pair of golden earrings. Ah Yee did not take them, sat down, and let her tears flow down her cheeks.

My father took the earrings and said, *"Hoe sim."* Have a heart. He told her to have pity on a woman who could not have children of her own; Ah Yee had so many she should be able to part with one. His brother was doing the family a favor by helping to raise Wan. There would be one less mouth to feed. To him, she was just another baby girl who could never carry on the family name, not a great loss, but to Ah Yee, she was her flesh and blood, and she was still breastfeeding her. The sudden separation was too much for her.

My uncle and aunt promised to have Fong and Boon visit them so Wan would always be in touch with us and they would make sure she knew Ah Yee was her real mother. There was no mention of an arrangement for Ah Yee to see her baby again. I assumed my uncle and aunt wanted to sever Ah Yee's relationship with Wan once and for all.

For many days after they left, Ah Yee's breasts were painfully engorged with milk. Squatting on the kitchen stone steps, she manually expressed her milk from her breasts to relieve her discomfort, letting it drip away along with her sorrow. She never wore those earrings. They made their way in and out of the pawnshop during times when we were short of money.

Later, my uncle and aunt adopted a boy, Ah Hong, and their family was now complete. Boon went down to Kuala Lumpur for his interview to train as a hospital assistant and stayed with them and thought my aunt was ferocious; she always had a cane beside her. While Wan had to do household chores, Ah Hong was their golden boy, treasured and loved. Although Boon did not see any ill treatment of Wan, he could not help but wonder if she had been adopted to be a maid for my aunt. When Thye went down to Kuala Lumpur to help with the household chores, she took the opportunity to tell Wan that Ah Yee was her real mother, and with that my uncle and aunt sent her packing.

We heard the news of our uncle's passing. Ah Yee never mentioned Wan again; her grief forever altered the fabric of her memory. Like her name, Wan, meaning cloud, floated into our family albeit through a long home delivery, and drifted out of it like a lonely cloud in the hot rainless trop-ical sky, forever erasing the hope of a reprieve of a good soaking rain. Somehow Ah Yee was able to go on with her life. Lian Hua, the youngest baby after Wan left, became her favorite and they grew very close.

My fond memory of Wan was when once she broke out in a rash, Ah Yee sent us to the field to collect as many vari-eties of wildflowers as we could while she fired up the stove with charcoal to heat up some water. I filled my skirt with flowers, disturbing the bees and the butterflies. When we came back sweaty and breathless, we dropped them into the tin basin of warm water. Ah Yee found the remains of an old wax umbrella, tore up the wax paper, and placed pieces of it in the water. Feverish, Wan was stripped naked, and the minute she touched the water, she cried, reaching out to Ah Yee, trying to get out of the bath. Ah Yee bathed her in the floral bath and we scooped handfuls of water to douse her. When Wan got used to the water temperature, she was happy in the metal tub, splashing her tiny chubby hands in the water, looking like a princess in her fabulous floral bath. The tepid bath brought her temperature down. In a few days, her rash slowly faded and she was her old playful self again.

Soon after losing Wan, Ah Yee gave birth to her seventh child, another girl, Yong, she arrived without much fanfare.

Looking back, I believe my aunt handed the pair of golden earrings as her way of expressing her gratitude to my mother for giving up her baby to a complete stranger to raise. I do not think she meant the earrings were compen-sation enough in exchange for a baby girl. It would have been more humane if my mother had been forewarned. My father did not feel the need to let her know, and during that post-war period, men made the decisions, and their women were to comply no matter how heart-wrenching it was going to be.

Because of Wan's adoption, I always had the lingering fear that the youngest baby girl might be the next target of my father's scheme. After all, he had to spend his hard-earned cash feeding her *see png*, dead rice, gaining nothing in return.

Part III
The girl
who taught herself
to fly

16

St. George's Girls' School
Aut viam inveniam aut faciam

At the end of form three, I sat for the Lower Certificate Examinations to determine whether I could go on to form four, and the results also guided the students into the pure science or the arts streams. Malaysia, a newly independent country, needed its share of science-based professionals such as engineers and doctors. The high-scoring students were streamed into the respected science stream.

Since our school did not have qualified teachers to teach the triple credit or pure science class, they only offered a double credit science course. During the previous year, Kuan May had been streamed into the arts class. When my turn came, my whole class (eighty percent were boys) was streamed into the science class, but we could only take a double credit science course despite our clamoring for a curriculum in triple credit science. To appease us, the department of education allowed the science teacher, Mr. Chen, who had only taught double credit science, to teach a triple credit course.

We spent our form four bumbling through what was assumed to be the curriculum for a triple credit science. But it soon became clear to us that Mr. Chen was not familiar with the course work and he stuck closely to the more familiar double credit science. Halfway through the year, in his exasperation, he just about admitted to us he was not sure whether he was teaching us enough to fulfill the requirements for the triple credit science course. I lost confidence in him. At the end of the year, three of us girls determined not to be bullied into accepting our fate, we applied for a transfer to the prestigious St. George's Girls' School.

St. George's Girls' School, or SGGS, was established by the Anglican missionaries in the late 1800s to educate girls from well-to-do families when its first informal classes were held in the Manse, home of the Anglican missionary, and taught by Mrs. Biggs, wife of Reverend L. Courtier Biggs. In 1885 a formal school was established and named after St. George, the patron saint of England. The school logo is a red crest with St. George on horseback slaying a dragon. In the early part of the twentieth century, the British government took over the running of the school briefly. After independence in 1957, it was handed over to the Malaya government and it continued to have a very good reputation in secondary school education during my time.

While waiting for my application to be processed, I continued into form five in the double credit science class. Two weeks passed; there was still no word from the department of education. I gathered enough courage and took a bus after school to meet with the headmistress of St. George's, a middle-aged woman reputed to be a stern, dragon lady. My heart pounded as I raised my hand to knock on the door. I heard a voice say, "Come in."

I walked in and stood at attention in front of the dragon lady's desk. She briefly looked up over the black rim of her glasses. Her jowls looked as menacing as a bulldog, and she did not invite me to sit down. Wearing a pink silk *cheong sum*, her moon-shaped face covered with pale pink foundation and powder, framed by a halo of black hair made stiff with hair spray, her lips painted a bright red, she reminded me of a Japanese geisha. I expected that at any moment she would whip out a fan to cover her face. I told her in a halting voice who I was and that I had applied to transfer to her school. There was no friendly smile, but she listened patiently. She had not heard from the education department and without their permission, she could not allow me to transfer.

That afternoon, determined to get an answer, with my stomach growling, I found my way to the education department at Penang Pier and boldly requested a meeting with the head. It was my first time walking alone into an imposing government office building. I climbed the three flights of stairs and sat in the waiting room, marveling at my own fearlessness.

I was sixteen years old.

After waiting for quite some time, I was ushered into the office. A quiet but imposing Malay man sat in his swivel chair with his hands folded on the desk. I stated my case. He remarked that I was fluent in English, and he was impressed by my determination and courage. I was encouraged and emboldened by his comments, and before we finished I reminded him there were two other students in the same predicament as me and they also wished to transfer. When I walked out of the building I was on cloud nine. The building swayed, it lasted for a second or so, and I assumed it was the adrenaline rush at having advocated for myself. The next day I learned there had been a small tremor felt by the island due to a seaquake originating in the Indian Ocean. It was as though the earth celebrated with me.

Within a week, all three of us received our papers for transfer to St. George's. The school's motto is *Aut viam inveniam aut faciam*. Where there's a will, there's always a way. It was printed on the glossy white covers of the exercise books emblazoned with the red crest. I had missed one whole year and a month of the pure science curriculum.

On our first day, our new form five classmates crowded around us, full of advice. They warned us about the dos and don'ts and the musts and mustn'ts dictated by Ma Ooi, the teacher who took upon herself to be the school disciplinarian. Our new skirts had to cover our knees and our red belts should not be wider than an inch. Ma Ooi's class monitor had a bob haircut, and her skirt reached down to her mid-calves. This was the era of mini-skirted Twiggy and wide belts were a craze. The girls put forth the theory that Ma Ooi, an old maid, wanted us to look dowdy and unattractive to the few male teachers around.

Soo Kion's main reason for the transfer was to be close to her twin sister. When the twins were born, her sister was ill and her parents sought the advice of a Chinese medium. He said that in order for the sick one to recover, the twins had to be raised separately. Reluctantly her parents gave the sick twin to a childless Malay couple who later moved away and they lost contact with them. When Soo Kion found out her twin sister was at St. George's, she longed to reunite with her. On our first day, she approached her; there was a definite resemblance. Her twin sister expressed no desire to have any kind of reunion with her or her family. Within a week, Soo Kion transferred back to our old school.

Going to a new school invoked plenty of anxiety and excitement. I had always kept my hair long and, for a long time, did not learn how to braid it. Before school, Ah Yee braided it into two long pigtails either hanging down or wrapped around my head. It made her mad when she was in a rush, yanking my hair as she braided it. Kuan May braided it on days when we had to go to school early.

When I came back from my first day at St. George's, I decided it was time to cut my hair short. I always considered myself an ugly duckling—awkward, chubby, and short. My hair, long, glossy, and wavy, was just about my only good asset, my redeeming feature, and crowning glory. Wavy hair was coveted by my sisters because they all had straight hair. Ah Yee had wavy and kinky hair from her visits to the perm parlor; my father's hair was short and wavy. When I approached her with a comb and a pair of scissors, she took a long wistful look at me and shook her head. She could not do it. Standing in front of the full-length mirror of her wardrobe, I carefully braided my hair into two long braids, took a deep breath, and cut them off close to my ears. I went back to the kitchen and showed her the two cut braids. She gasped. I left her no choice, and she had to trim my hair.

I went to school with my wavy hair grazing just above my shoulders, wearing my new uniform: a starchy white frock with a red belt with the crest sewn on the left side of the blouse. It was all very smart compared to my old school uniform: a brown pinafore cinched with a brown belt over a dull creamy linen blouse. Ma Ooi emerged from her classroom, and before I could slip through the French doors, she spotted me. She had her class monitor summon me for her inspection. My classmates stared at me with looks of pity and dismay. With leaden feet, I followed the class monitor, pulling on my skirt, hoping to add inches to its length.

Ma Ooi sat on a metal chair wielding a ruler. She asked me if I was one of the new girls. I nodded. Then she went on a spiel about discipline in the school and that it was not a place for fashion but a place for study. Zeroing in on the length of my skirt, which just managed to cover my knobby knees, she sadistically raised my hem with her ruler. I passed her length requirement, but just barely. She had me undo my belt and measured its width. My mother had made it exactly one inch wide and so it did not present a problem for me.

Then she flicked her ruler at my newly cut wavy hair and said, "Why all these curls? Your hair should be cut close to your ears or tied into a ponytail. Are you trying to be seductive and attract attention to yourself?"

My downcast eyes settled on the long slit of her *cheong sum*, which revealed a big patch of her unsightly, leathery thigh up close to her hip. I waited for her to dismiss me. She asked her monitor to see to it that I tied up my hair.

At home, I begged Ah Yee to cut my hair shorter, but she refused. It was too short to be put into a single ponytail and so I went to school with two, feeling like a primary school girl. The monitor approved. I spent the rest of my form five year avoiding Ma Ooi.

—

A new school year called for new textbooks, a real worry for me. The books for higher forms were more expensive. Right after school, I took my list of books straight to the used book stores in Chulia Street, all of them owned by Tamil Indians, before throngs of students descended with the same mission on their minds.

I ran into a couple of students I knew, silently acknowledging one another. One of them was Asoka, a petite, quiet, and hardworking Indian girl from Jelutong Secondary School, always wearing her hair in two long pigtails. The other was Suraniya, a fair, tall, and cheerful Chinese girl adopted by an Indian family. That was unusual because very few Chinese families would give their children away to a family of a darker race. Her Indian parents doted on her, and she owned many assortments of beautiful *sari*. Both Asoka and Suraniya wore a *bindi*, a black dot on their foreheads indicating their unmarried status.

The storekeepers climbed up wooden ladders, searching high and low in the bookcases for my books, looking for the latest editions. Sometimes I was not so lucky and had to decide whether to spend the money on an old edition which might be totally outdated. They had a no return policy. The afternoon of searching was exhausting. I went home with some of the books and had to figure out how much I would have to spend to buy the rest, new. Occasionally I was able to buy books from the older students.

I borrowed my classmates' new books and compared the editions. Sometimes there were so many changes I had to look through chapter by chapter, page by page, and line by line, noting the changes in the margins of my old textbooks, making me lose faith in the validity of the information. I hugged the new books to my chest, inhaling the fresh smell, wishing they were mine.

For Suraniya, her search for old books was no longer necessary. One day she walked past our house adorned in a brightly colored and intricate *sari*, a gold filigree scarf covered her hair. Her adoring Indian parents walked beside her. She was soon to be married and had no need for more school. The next time I saw her she was walking arm in arm with her short Indian husband, and this time she had a red *bindi* on her fair forehead.

When I joined my classmates at the new school, I had already missed a whole year of form four and a month's worth of form five class work. During our first week, Lan Fong, the other transfer, and I borrowed notebooks on biology, chemistry, and physics from the girls and copied the various experiments they had performed in the form four class. There were numerous pages of notes, illustrations, dissections, and graphs that had to be hand-copied and then studied on our own. The pure science curriculum was far more detailed and in-depth than what my form four science teacher had taught us.

Our old school hadn't offered calculus to form four students. Lan Fong's sister was in form six, and every afternoon for two months, she tutored us in calculus. This was imperative because Mrs. Lin, the math teacher, was about to return from her maternity leave, and from the girls' description, she was a terror. The substitute teacher, Mrs. Wong, had only been reading from the calculus book and was not in the habit of calling on the girls to do problems on the board.

When Mrs. Lin returned, the atmosphere in the class was instantly transformed. The girls had their noses buried in their books. I was glad Lan Fong and I sat in the last seats in the third row as far away as one could get from the teacher's desk. She was widget thin despite having just delivered her firstborn. She peered at the class over the rim of her glasses, with her nasal and irritatingly whiny voice, she made us repeat after her while she read a problem in the book. When she chose a girl to solve a problem, she had her repeat the question verbatim before she could provide the answer. She was so hung up on us repeating the questions, she spent little time teaching us calculus. What we learned of calculus, we learned through Lan Fong's sister and on our own.

Mr. Chan, my form five teacher who taught us English and English literature, was dubbed the most eligible bachelor at St. George's. There was not much of a contest since there were only four male teachers; five when Mr. Chin, our physics teacher, joined the teaching force. Mr. Chuah, the bespectacled chemistry teacher, nicknamed "the blinking idiot," had a nervous tick that caused him to blink at frequent intervals. He was already married so he really did not qualify as a bachelor. Besides, his face was prominently filled with scars from acne that troubled him in his youth. The even-tempered, patient Malay teacher, Mr. Ibrahim, had a quivery, soft-spoken voice. He was as thin as a rail; his pants hung loosely on his skinny waist and were prevented from slipping off by his suspenders. Often at the receiving end of practical jokes concocted by the girls, he bore them all with a wry sense of humor. Mr. Lee had a shot at the title for the most eligible bachelor. He was young, clean-cut, happy, kind, good-looking, and a sports teacher. But Mr. Chan, a fixture at St. George's for many years, had gone to school in Liverpool, England, and trumped Mr. Lee due to his English accent. A sharp dresser, he often wore a pink Oxford shirt. His thin physique and a haggard look of melancholia and aloneness aroused the mother's instinct among the girls, and they found him irresistibly attractive. Rosana, one of the Malay girls, went so far as to say, "Oh what a sad look he has. Poor thing. He needs to be taken care of."

To the girls, Mr. Chan was someone they both adored for his mind as well as his looks, despite being a chain smoker—a packet of Marlboro cigarettes always sat in his shirt pocket. They were willing to overlook this, believing they could correct this bad ingrained habit with their long-suffering love. He could not wait to light up as soon as he stepped out of the classroom. When we had back-to-back English and English literature classes, he excused himself and went to the staff room to smoke. We could hear his smoker's cough long before he arrived in class. The movie, *To Sir, with Love*, came out just around this time, which made the girls even crazier over their form teacher. The racial undertone of the movie resonated with the multi-racial environment in which we were all brought up.

Sue was a prefect in our class and had cropped curly dark hair framing her round, fair, and friendly face. Her parents established and ran a Chinese school on the island, and she was chauffeured to school every day, unlike most of us who had to walk to the bus stop and wait for the bus under the shade of the flame of the forest trees during the hottest part of the day. She was Mr. Chan's favorite and was well aware of his special attention and sat through the class period with her head buried in her book, hardly raising it unless he asked her a question.

Once a month, Mr. Chan handed her *The Times Literary Supplement* for her to choose interesting articles to be posted on the bulletin board at the back of the class. None of us could read any of the posted articles because, to prevent petty thefts, we were not allowed to remain in the classroom during recess. Mr. Chan was not aware of this rule. Even when we took turns keeping watch for Ma Ooi, we were too fearful of being caught to really absorb any information.

Our first-in-class assigned essay was "My first day at school." Most people would write about their first day at school in kindergarten, but it dawned on me I could just as well write about my first day at St. George's.

When Lan Fong and I first arrived, two groups of girls immediately confronted us at separate times. The first group was the "clever girls" with good marks, and they sat near the front of the class; the second, a much larger one made up of the average students. The rest of the students kept to themselves and did not belong to either of the groups. The representatives of both groups gave their ultimatum that we had to choose to join either one of them or else be shunned. Lan Fong refused to give her answer and buried her head in her textbook, but I told them I did not want to belong to either. From that day on, they ignored us. It was not until later in the year when Lan Fong and I excelled in class and showed them we were just as capable as them in achieving good marks that they began to see us as their competitors and rivals.

In the forty-five minutes I had to write my essay, I recounted the girls' ultimatum and how it was different from my former school; we got along without such pettiness and cliques. As I wrote my essay, I felt feverish and a few itchy blisters developed on my neck, forehead, and upper arms. Lan Fong took a look at them and told me I was coming down with the chickenpox.

When I returned home, I skipped lunch and went straight to sleep. I woke up in the sweltering heat later that afternoon with many more blisters erupting on my body. I stayed home for the next two weeks but only missed one week of school because one of the two weeks was the Chinese New Year holiday and school was closed for the celebration. Lan Fong brought home my essay. I had received a mark of 69 out of 100. Shocked and disappointed, I had never received any mark below 85. Later the girls explained that Mr. Chan was a hard grader and any mark in the 60s was considered a very good grade. On the last page, he concurred with my keen observation on the divisiveness of the class.

In our English literature class, we read aloud a play about Alexander the Great. Mr. Chan assigned Sue to be the mother of the conqueror; Rosana to be Roxana, Alexander's wife; and himself, Alexander the Great. I wondered why he did not assign Sue to be Alexander's wife but it soon became clear that as Alexander's mother, Sue had to address him multiple times with terms of endearment. I could hear the hesitation in her voice while the girls sitting at the back giggled themselves silly. He looked up at them, coughed, and cleared his throat. This made them giggle even more. Sue sat across from his desk and had her head lowered into her book. I was sure she wished she could disappear from the surface of the earth.

Mr. Chan calmly looked down at her, cleared his throat, and said, "Go on."

We later read *Macbeth*. It was a good thing Cambridge University, that set up our curriculum for O-Levels, did not assign *Romeo and Juliet* for our Shakespearean play. It would have been far more discomfiting.

When the class ended, Miss Yeoh, our geography teacher stepped into the classroom, and the girls were still laughing. She was easily the prettiest teacher in the whole of St. George's—young, slender, fair, and vivacious. Her dresses were modern and airy, well-suited to the tropical humidity, and she tied her hair up with a long colorful scarf. She had gone to school in Melbourne, Australia, and this fact lent an aura of mystery to her whole persona. Because she was single, it would have been most appropriate and romantic to pair her with Mr. Chan. However, they always greeted each other formally and carried themselves with an air of professionalism.

One day the girls spotted Mr. Chan driving away with one of the schoolgirls in his maroon MG sports car. Rumor had it that he had taken this girl under his wing because of her troubled past. The same girl also started coming to school every day in the sports car with him. Broken-hearted, many of the girls would gladly have exchanged places with her.

While the girls were shy and incommunicative in Mr. Chan's class, they were rowdy and unruly in Mr. Chuah's chemistry class. A married man and not as handsome as Mr. Chan, he was not strict with the girls and let them get away with murder. We performed experiments in the laboratory involving the interaction of different chemicals. One of the gases was hydrogen sulfide with the smell of rotten eggs. It sat in a big bell jar in the corridor. He had a set of old notebooks with lesson plans which he used year after year. The girls were tempted to steal his notes to see if he was still able to teach without them.

For a while, we did not have a physics teacher until the vacancy was filled by Mr. Chin, a recent graduate from the University of Malaya in Kuala Lumpur. We all stood at attention and said good morning to him when he first walked into the classroom. He looked as if he had just rolled out of bed—his rumpled white shirt was not tucked in completely into his black pants and his hair seemed to have not seen a comb in a while. The girls learned that he had gone to a Chinese secondary school. They assumed his command of English would not be as good as Mr. Chan and quickly concluded he could be bullied. It turned out his English was exceptionally good, and he was an excellent and knowledgeable teacher. As his shirt-tail was always out of his pants, the class decided to play "pin the tail on the teacher." The girl sitting closest to the blackboard tried to attach a long white handkerchief to the back of his pants. As he paced before the blackboard, she reached forward with the cloth. We held our collective breath and then burst into giggles. Befuddled, he could not figure out what was so funny until he caught her in action and scolded us for wasting our parents' tuition fees by not paying attention in class.

The feared Miss Cheah was our biology teacher, tall and with a commanding presence. Like Miss Yeoh, she had her graduate degree from Australia. It was rumored that her fiancé had jilted her, so she returned to Malaya to teach at St. George's. She poured her heart out, preparing us for our O-Levels but at the same time, she seemed also to be gung-ho on torturing us. She gave us pop quizzes a couple times a week on random topics, including those that were covered in form four. Lo and behold, during our first class with her, she told us to put away all our books and take out our exercise book for a pop quiz. The girls groaned while she laughed gleefully. Lan Fong and I did not do too badly as she posed questions on topics from form four—we were familiar with them since we had just copied the notes.

"This was well done," she said to me when she passed back our marked exercise books.

We spent an inordinate amount of time dissecting toads in her class. The evenings before our laboratory, my sisters and I went to an open field. We kicked the wet dewy grass, disturbing the toads and catching them with our bare hands when they hopped out. We put them in bottles covered with paper poked with holes for air.

The next day I handed the toads over to the laboratory technicians. Most of the girls from the clever group lived in the city and they could not find any toads to catch; they depended on us living in the outskirts of Georgetown. When it came time for our dissection, they made a beeline for the big bell jar of chloroformed toads and picked the biggest for themselves, leaving the smaller ones for us. Once I asked the laboratory technician to save me a particularly big toad, a mother of all toads, but she could not make the girls obey her.

In June we took our mid-year examination. When all our marks were tallied, I scored the second highest in the class. This caught the clever girls' attention.

Our class monitor, Wei Ni, left for higher studies in Australia. The class ran an election for another class monitor. Three names were nominated including Liling, the first girl, the leader of the group of clever girls. Surprisingly the group of girls with average marks nominated me, a new girl, and the third nominee was Rosana. We stepped out while the class conducted their election. I was elected overwhelmingly, much to the consternation of Liling and her supporters. As a class monitor, I had to keep the class quiet in between periods, collect homework and bring it to the staff room, assign duties to the girls, and make sure they all stood at attention to greet the teachers at the beginning of each period. For that honor, I wore a blue enamel badge with the words "Class Monitor" engraved on it. That was the fastest boost in status for me, in less than six months in a new school.

At the end of form five, I became the new first girl. My total marks were higher than Liling's. She was toppled from the pedestal. Her entourage of clever girls was shocked into speechlessness. She displayed her displeasure by plunking her books on her chair with a loud bang. But to her credit, she congratulated me on my accomplishment. Miss Cheah did not mince her words; she told the girls they should be ashamed of themselves, beaten by a girl transferred into St. George's. What she really meant was they had been beaten by a girl who transferred from a non-prestigious school.

We had more pressing matters on our minds; we had to be ready to sit for our O-Levels.

There were fifty students in my form five class, the majority were Chinese, two Indian, two Malay (one of whom was ethnically Chinese but was adopted by a Malay family), and two Sikh girls, Akbal and Surinder Kaur. They had the same surname, but they were not related.

Akbal invited me to her home. They lived in a semi-detached house. Her father lay on a charpoy with strong ropes strung together as support in the courtyard. Akbal's mother wore a *salwar kameez*, a baggy loosely fitting pant with an ankle cuff or *ponche*. Over the baggy pant, she had an embroidered top reaching to her mid-calves. Her hair was tied up in a bun and over her shoulders was draped a gossamer scarf.

Both Kaurs were slender and tall; Akbal was more talkative and outspoken. They kept their hair all done up in pony or pigtails; their custom forbade them to cut their hair. The Sikh men also kept their hair long, tied up in a knot, and wrapped up in a turban. What struck me as impressive was that these two girls knew for sure they wanted to be doctors and they never once wavered from their decision. Akbal's parents were supportive of her, a mere girl, to go to medical school and make something of herself. At least in Penang, women Punjabi doctors were not uncommon. How it came about that in Punjabi culture it was acceptable for women to go to medical school was a mystery to me. Years later both Akbal and Surinder went to medical school and became doctors.

The fate of the women in my life, slowly unraveled for me. Marriage seemed to dominate the lives of many women, including Ah Yee, with no freedom to choose. Forced out of school prematurely, they had no other way to elevate their status in society and become independent financially, slated to a life caring for a brood of children, bringing them up in a world that they hoped might be vastly different from their own.

Fong trained to be a nurse, opening a path for her to have a choice in a career and not fall headlong into marriage and children. The image of the tall, female Punjabi doctor remained etched in my mind. I had once met Meng Kee's boss, a female Chinese professor at the Universiti Sains Malaysia in Penang—a single woman who owned her house and drove a car, a rare thing for a woman to do then. These two professional women reminded me that they had arrived at their positions through higher education, undoubtedly aided by family encouragement and financial support.

I was well aware that I had neither.

My parents did not know about my year-end report card, or that their child won many awards in the school. I had no doubt they were too poor to send me to a university when I completed my secondary school education, despite my father's boastful babbling of sending me to Australia.

Was there still a glimmer of hope for me to get myself educated and out of the cycle of poverty? Would there be a chance for me to carve out my own destiny?

I looked at the past year of success—getting a transfer to St. George's Girls' School in my determination to take the triple credit science course. I had proved to myself that I was capable of overcoming barriers and obstacles when I had the tenacious will to do so.

Aut viam inveniam aut faciam.

17

Squatters and eminent domain

I t seemed to be our kismet to be pursued and chased away by road construction.

It was in the Rifle Range orchard when the developer built many blocks of houses on the land behind our home, plowing through the badminton court Ah Wee built; the green field overgrown with wildflowers was long gone and the bees and butterflies disappeared. One of the roads in the development ended abruptly behind our house, looking as though it wished to run through it to join the road in front. The strip of land next to our house was fast becoming a thoroughfare, people using it to connect the new community to the old one. We lost the privacy we used to enjoy; the quiet bliss of the countryside had been invaded by more houses and people.

In the end, my father sold the developer the orchard, bought a piece of land in Dragon's Tail, and built a brand new house with walls of corrugated sheets and zinc roofing. There a road that originated in a cluster of houses in Kampong Melayu abruptly ended at the edge of the development. Our house sat along a dirt road connected to a tarmac road leading to Ayer Itam with a busy market and several Buddhist temples including the island's famous Kek Lok Si Temple, the Temple of Supreme Bliss. Secretly we hoped the road that led to nowhere was not going to continue and run through our house as the road had at the fruit orchard. The only reassurance was that there was plenty of land in front of our house. But still, this remained a threat staring at us every day.

When we moved to Dragon's Tail from the fruit orchard, my father did not hook up our new house with electricity or water. There were municipal sources of electricity and water but either he could not afford them or he was again short-changed by the contractors.

Kuan May and I burned Ah Yee's altar candle votives for the first few nights to study. They burned too quickly to provide light for a reasonable period of time. It drove Ah Yee crazy seeing them burn; to her it was equivalent to throwing money into a fire. Then she bought a kerosene lamp which cast a dim light. We hurried to take our baths in daylight. God be with the person who had to take the kerosene lamp to light her way in the dark outhouse lest she be swallowed whole by the squatting hole.

I read by the kerosene lamp in bed, deep into the night. There were times when I fell asleep while the lamp was still burning. Once I knocked it over after falling asleep and would have set the house on fire were it not for the fact that Kuan May woke up in time to notice the roaring flames arising from the lamp. Despite a stern lecture from her, I continued the habit of reading with the kerosene lamp next to my pillow but exercised greater caution.

During our long stay in the orchard, my father had updated our water supply from the well to piped water. Now we were back to well water, and the well belonged to our neighbors who lived in a shed of rusty corrugated tin and *nipa* palms behind our house. We drew water every day for our baths and filled the tank up for Ah Yee.

Our neighbors, Mr. and Mrs. Chin, were like Mr. and Mrs. Jack Pratt of Mother Goose. Mrs. Chin was fat, draped in a loud pink flowery *sarong* worn over her voluminous breasts with her round shoulders exposed while Mr. Chin was tall, dark, haggard, hunched, and skinny, wearing only skimpy boxers and flip-flops. His bare chest showed his skeletal rib cage, and he was constantly hampered by a smoker's cough. Mrs. Chin sat on a low rocking chair outside her house, fanning herself and prattling all day, hen-pecking her husband who catered to her demands. Once seated she had a hard time getting up to move around.

They would let us use the well if we could help pay for the rope to draw water. This had to be replaced frequently because it wore off at a good clip. When Ah Yee did not have the money to replace a broken rope, we tied the broken ends. But Mrs. Chin swore and used foul words that made Ah Yee blush. The knot made it difficult to pull the rope over the pulley. Like the knot, our relationship with the neighbors was not a smooth one.

Postwar construction was booming. A few years after we moved to Dragon's Tail, the forest of cashew trees in front of our home was bulldozed and the ground was broken for more new homes. In the evenings, my father and Ah Wee sat close together, murmuring about the possibility of moving. The term "eminent domain" was thrown around. It seemed my father had to accept what the government gave him based on the estimated value of our home. In the course of the investigation, it became clear the builders had built our home on government land, making us squatters. He had been cheated yet again. In the end, he did not receive much for the house.

Years later when we revisited Dragon's Tail, the road that had abruptly ended at the edge of the development continued right over the well and ran through the ground where our old house had been. The Chins still lived in their shed, now set next to the new road, open and exposed to the public eye. I wondered where they got their water supply now that the well was buried under the tarmac; I was glad we had moved away from this house.

Our parents made us pack our meager belongings of books and clothes. The movers would move us while we were in school and we were to make our way to our new home after school was over. All morning I had difficulty concentrating, wondering what type of home we would be moving to, hoping that it would be a decent place with running water and electricity.

In the hot, sultry early afternoon, Kuan May and I stepped off the green Lim Seng Seng bus at a different bus stop from our old home and crossed the busy Ayer Itam Road amidst the black diesel fumes spilling from the tailpipes of the departing bus, to the entrance of Hye Keat Estate, marked by a stone bridge spanning a small brook. The restaurant where my father ran a stall was next to it. A gigantic bottle of Coca-Cola sat on the rooftop of the restaurant, neither Kuan May nor I had ever tasted coke; an ice-cold one would have been lovely then.

We walked in the heat for half a mile through stucco terraced homes with private gardens surrounded by metal fences and gates, festooned with bougainvillea and hibiscus. With fewer tall and shady trees, Hye Keat Estate was more open and sunnier than Dragon's Tail. The general nice appearance of the houses bolstered my spirit, and in my heart, I hoped our new home would be just as beautiful. We reached the end of the road, which ran right smack into a temple, a gated imposing structure with stone lions standing guard at the entrance. The inside looked quiet, dark, and cool. We made a sharp right turn and reached our new home on our right.

Two families shared this terraced house and our part of the house was on the left, set a few feet from the tarmac road with a dusty gravel path leading to it. To my great disappointment, there was no fence, gate, or enclosed garden. The stucco house was painted white while the doors and windows were a bright blue. It was divided right down the middle by a cement wall, but there was no ceiling or wall from the rafters to the roof between the two families. The corrugated tin roof engulfed the house in sweltering heat during the day, and at night, it continued to emit the absorbed heat as it crackled and settled, making sleep uncomfortable. Our neighbors, who had the mirror image of our rented home, ran a sundry store. A few hundred yards from our house was a bigger and fancier general store carrying a greater variety of goods; a major competitor for our neighbor mom-and-pop store.

From the front patio, we walked into a small sitting room. This was where Kuan May and I studied late into the night under the glare and the droning of a fluorescent light. Ah

Fatt, our neighbor, was busy on his side of the wall, doing his accounts on the abacus, clacking the beads. His radio was on, and at midnight, the program ended first with a Chopin nocturne followed by the national anthem. The tune of the nocturne always made me feel sad. Kuan May and I did not linger long after the witching hour.

The hallway was to the side of the house closer to our neighbors and three bedrooms opened off of it. We all squeezed into the first bedroom. Ah Wee, who remained single, occupied the second one; and my parents took the third. Fong and Boon lived in the nursing hostel. The long hall ended in the kitchen with a big cement stove. The bathroom sat in a corner, and the area between it and the kitchen proper was without a roof, letting in welcoming daylight, making this room the most cheerful part of the house. When it rained, the stove, set off a few feet from the open area, would get wet. Ah Yee had a miserable time keeping the fire going. Our bathroom had a concrete container for water, but this time we had running water—a refreshing change. Our outhouse sat at the back, a flushing toilet was still a pipe dream.

Under the open roof, Ah Wee built a two-floor chicken coop sitting on stilts so that Ah Yee could spray water directly into it, washing away the waste products into the drain and the sun would take care of the drying. Every night the chickens had a choice of staying on the first or the second floor of their upgraded condominium. The ducks took the first floor as it was unwieldy for them to climb up the steps. Ah Yee stopped keeping turkeys or geese. Our old gander died at Dragon's Tail of old age.

It did not take us long to put away our clothes and books. In the midst of unpacking and the excitement of a new home, we did not notice our cat, Tiger, was missing until later in the evening. Ah Yee was very quiet about it. She had never wanted to keep a cat since she had to set aside money to feed it. My father decided to abandon Tiger. Dragon's Tail was at least three miles from our new home, crisscrossed by many busy roads. Saddened by the loss of our cat, Fong, Boon, Kuan May, and I walked to our old home to look for him, even venturing to ask our former quarrelsome neighbors whether they had by any chance seen Tiger. Ah Yee had all her fowls accounted for. Unlike a cat, the chickens and ducks were Ah Yee's bank account; they were all carefully carted off in the lorry during the move.

A few days passed and one evening we saw a scrawny cat picking his way furtively along the hedges just beyond our neighbor's house. It looked like Tiger but we could not be sure. We called his name, and he started bouncing toward us. Indeed it was Tiger. He nuzzled in our arms, thin and gaunt. How he found his way to our new house was a mystery. Even Ah Yee was impressed, and he was welcomed.

During the day, Ah Yee let her chickens and ducks outdoors after they were fed, initially in a wire mesh enclosure and, when she thought they were familiar with their new surroundings, she let them have their freedom to roam around the backyards of our neighbors. They were hens, concubines of the rooster, being herded by him proudly. In the heat of the tropical sun, they snoozed under the bushes or took dust baths. When they were thirsty, there was a brook conveniently close by.

In the evening when feeding time came, Ah Yee called out to her chickens. The rooster invariably straightened his neck, held his head high, and cocked his ear to listen. When she called again, and it was deemed by him that it was unmistakably her voice, a series of cooing sounds emerged from his throat, coaxing the hens to follow him home. As he strutted homeward, he looked around making sure every single one of his clan followed him.

When Ah Yee fed them, he behaved like a perfect gentleman, letting the hens eat first before he took even a single peck. No wonder he was skinny, but his coat always had a healthy sheen. During the day when the chickens were left to forage, the rooster offered live earthworms that he caught in his beak to the hens, dividing them by swiping them on the ground.

In the morning, after the chickens were already fed and let out, I used the backyard as a shortcut to and from the bus stop on my way to school, frightening and scattering them. Of course, I promptly forgot about it. After a long morning at school, I walked home in the hot sun, taking the shortcut, deep in my own thoughts about the lunch that was waiting for me. Then I heard a fluttering behind me. I turned, squinting against the bright sun, and saw a huge flying mass coming toward me. The rooster landed on my shoulders and pecked my head. I shrugged him off, swinging my school bag wildly as I made my get-away. But I did not get very far before I heard another flutter and felt the stinging on my calves from his beak. I was only safe when I ran into the kitchen. Outside the back door, the rooster with his angry red wattle, strutted proudly, guarding the door.

I stopped taking the shortcut for a while. When I did I made sure I checked for the rooster. If he was close by I swung my school bag at him, making a lot of noise to frighten him off. After that near massacre, I had a healthy respect for him. Eventually, we reached a truce. I glowered at him and he cockled from a safe distance.

My little brother Beng came home one day, eyes wide with excitement, telling us that one of our neighbors had bought a huge box with a screen and Beng had been there to watch *The Lone Ranger*. He galloped through the house, blaring the "William Tell Overture." The box attracted many of the neighboring children. They went to the sitting room of the house every day to watch the show. I was dying to take a look but was too shy. When Ah Yee asked me to go to the neighbor's house to bring Beng home for dinner, I craned my neck trying to get a glimpse of the magic box. The television had trumped Ah Fatt's radio.

The concept of renting was new to Ah Yee. In addition to money for our daily meal, she had to set aside rent money for the landlady who came to collect it once a month. Happily, Ah Wee helped her with the rent. The landlady was a heavy-set woman resplendent in silk and jewelry. After stepping out of her tinted air-conditioned limo, while her chauffeur waited for her, she swaggered into our house ostensibly displaying her wealth. Filling up the whole house with her voluminous presence, she loomed large next to my diminutive mother.

Strutting like a peacock, she conducted a thorough inspection of our sparse furniture, our new matching set of powder-blue Formica table, chairs, and cupboard in the sitting room recently purchased by Fong and Boon. I was sure she coveted them and would have taken them as payment if Ah Yee could not pay her rent. In the cupboard were my treasured books; *Alice in Wonderland* and *Through the Looking Glass*. Finally, she went straight to her mission of collecting rent, "*Or lui boh?*" Do you have the money? When Ah Yee did not have enough money to pay her, she threatened eviction. She grudgingly gave Ah Yee a few more days and left in a huff, yelling loud enough for all the neighbors to hear we could not pay our rent, humiliating us.

Ah Yee grew apprehensive when the time came for the landlady to collect the rent. The landlady varied the time of day or day of the week she came to collect. When we spotted her black polished limousine, we ran to tell Ah Yee. Dropping whatever she was doing, she hurried to her bedroom, put a blouse over her *sarong*, released her thick, black, kinky hair from the rubber band, and combed it. She hid the rent money in the folds of her *sarong*, determined to hang onto some of it to see the family through the month. She begged the landlady to accept part of the rent and to come back for the rest later in the month. More often than not, the landlady was insistent on collecting all of it. Unwillingly, Ah Yee handed it over and then asked for some repairs around the house. The landlady threatened to rent it out to someone else, effectively silencing Ah Yee. She was nicer to our neighbor, Ah Fatt, who was in a much better position to pay his rent on time. His part of the house was in good shape and did not need repairing.

All eight of us slept on mats on the wooden floor in the first bedroom; the baby and sometimes another younger sibling slept in the same bed with my parents. We lay with our feet in the same direction from the oldest to the youngest, packed like sardines. Like our Malay house, the wooden floor was infested with bed bugs. I woke up in the middle of the night with long beads of welts on my arms. When Ah Yee could afford to heat up an extra kettle of water, pouring hot water along the cracks in the wooden floor to kill the bugs, we all had a few restful nights. But this respite did not last long. Within a week the eggs hatched and we were eaten alive again.

In October the heavy monsoon rain came pelting on the corrugated tin roof, sounding like the hooves of galloping horses, growing louder and then receding. The first time it rained, the deafening pounding woke up the younger siblings. They cried for Ah Yee. Raindrops came in through the long slit-like window under which Kuan May slept. She jumped up to close it. Soon the younger ones drifted off to sleep. I lay awake, my eyes wide open, waiting for the rain to leak through the roof and drip onto our bodies as it had in the Malay house where Ah Yee placed buckets to catch the raindrops with the "ping, ping, thud, thud" noises that continued through the night.

Miracle of miracles, the roof did not leak!

During the nights of the monsoon season, the tin roof was tested by the forceful wind. Half of the roof flew up from the rafters into the sky, staying momentarily in mid-air, flirting with the wind before finally collapsing on top of the house with a loud bang. The sky was visible from where I lay. On a rainless night, a few stars twinkled. Before long another gust of wind came, lifting the roof, inviting it to join in the dance. Many nights I worried about us sleeping under the sky with no roof over our heads. The younger ones got used to the monsoon; their chests rose and fell with their breathing, with a wheezy whisper from Beng. When it was all over, the roof was back on top of the house, quiet and serene, as though it had never taken part in any of the mischief of the night. The winds retreated to their place of origin. Ah Yee said they resided in the four cardinal directions. In the monsoon season, they joined forces and came out in full force.

When the wind stopped blowing, I got up and picked my way over the sleeping bodies of my siblings. In the shadows, cockroaches scurried on the bare floor. I reached the door and stepped down onto the cold cement floor and felt my way to the sitting room. The wall clock ticked. Not a sound issued from Ah Fatt's house, except for a series of chapping calls from the *cicak*, the house geckos, crawling on our common wall. They seemed to chide Kuan May and me when we stayed up late to study. The moon shone through an open window onto a big puddle collected on the floor. I walked over to close it, listening to the chirping of the crickets celebrating the end of the storm.

The next time the landlady came to collect the rent, Ah Yee let her know about the dancing roof. She went outside, walked around the house, stood across the street, shading her eyes from the sun while peering at the roof, and concluded that it was strong enough to withstand any monsoon wind. Of course, she only came when the weather was not stormy. The roof in one corner of our house was not tethered down and it continued to be lifted off the rafters during a windy storm, but the roof over Ah Fatt's portion of the rental property was as usual not affected.

—

On the Nine Emperor Festival, which was on the first to the ninth day of the ninth month of the Chinese Lunar calendar, my father took a rare day off. Since we lived close by the Cheng Kon Sze on the 1002 stairs hill, we, along with hundreds of devotees, hiked up the steep granite steps snaking up to the temple where the air was cooler. The smell of incense burning and the continuous tick-tock on the prayer bowls filled the air. Water from a mountain stream piped through a bamboo stem into a stone was cold and refreshing. The monks served a vegetarian meal of fried noodles, one of the best I ever tasted.

The images of the gods here were less forbidding than those in the bigger and more touristy Kek Lok Si Temple, a few miles away. At that temple, the red-faced Guan Gong was one such massive statue at least two stories tall, dressed in a dragon robe and carrying a Guan Dao sword. He had my family's generational name and I loved to think we had a distant tie to royalty as he was the brother of the first emperor, Liu Bei of the Kingdom of Shu, and played a significant role in establishing the kingdom. He is still respected as the epitome of loyalty, moral qualities, righteousness, and worshiped by the Chinese people today as the God of War.

In this modest temple, my father burned incense and joss sticks, mouthing a prayer to the gods. He stuck the joss sticks into the urn, then he knelt down and touched his forehead on the tiled floor. He had not been blessed with good fortune in a long while, what with us being chased away from our own home. After he was cheated of his pension, instead of owning an orchard and a home, he was reduced to being a renter, with no land or house to call his own.

The next day was just an ordinary day. My father went back to scratching for a living, running his food stall. The road ahead of him remained lonely, long, and arduous.

18

The race riots of 1969

On May 13, 1969, there were murmurings of unrest in the capital, Kuala Lumpur, circulating in the class. Our teacher asked us to gather our books into our bags, then she dismissed us in groups, barring us from using the route at the back of the school that cut across the Maternity and Penang General Hospitals. School officials herded us to the front of the school to Macalister Road where the Chief Minister of Penang had his residence. The driveway in front of the school's tall clock tower was bustling with private cars of well-to-do families whisking their children away. Unfortunately for me, it meant a long and circuitous bus ride to the Penang Pier taking me farther away from my home, and then walking fifteen minutes in the heat to the bus terminal in Georgetown to catch a second bus that called for an additional bus fare. I was more worried about having to dish out the additional fare. I fished in my pocket to make sure I had enough change.

Sue's chauffeur arrived to take her home. Her sister, who attended another school, was already in the car. Neither the headmistress nor the teachers explained to us what was actually happening and why they were afraid. At the bus stop, students became agitated as the bus took a long time to come and when it did, it was almost full. Fear was etched in the eyes of the passengers. I finally boarded a city council bus, standing all the way to Weld Quay. In normal times, this scenic route would be a fun trip as it ran along Peel Avenue lined with regal stately palm trees, through the rich residential area with beautiful colonial homes. But I was not in the mood. Something was really wrong and I did not know what.

At the pier, the sun was at its peak, and amidst the grime and fumes of the busy bus station, I connected with my second bus heading toward home. The bus was again jam-packed. It snaked through the center of Georgetown on Penang Road and found its way to the bus stop where I normally would catch my bus if I were not barred from taking the back route. It took almost twice as long to get home that afternoon. Ah Yee was relieved to see me. I was surprised to see my father. He had closed his stall early. He had no choice; the restaurant sent everyone home.

Ah Wee came home pedaling his bike using only one leg. While biking through a Malay *kampong,* the Malays attacked him and hit him on the leg. Using his uninjured leg to turn the paddle, he quickly took a detour to Batu Lanchang Road through the Chinese cemetery. Blood trailed from his injured leg as he limped into the house. Then we learned that the race riots of May 13, 1969, had started that afternoon. Now I understood why my teacher did not want us to wait for the bus right across from the Malay *kampong;* the riot that erupted in Kuala Lumpur was between the Chinese and the Malays.

In May 1969 the opposition Democratic Action Party with a large Chinese following and the Gerakan won the elections over the ruling Alliance coalition headed by the United Malays National Organization (UMNO). The winning party obtained a permit from the police for a victory parade through a fixed route in the capital. Unfortunately, the unruly crowd deviated from the route and went through a Malay village of Kampong Bahru, hurling verbal insults. The next day the offending party offered apologies, but the opposing party, UMNO, decided to organize a counter-parade. Before the start of the parade, the gathering Malay crowd heard a rumor that the Chinese had attacked some Malays while *en route* to the procession. The angry crowd exacted revenge by killing two passing Chinese motorists, inciting the riots of May 13. The riots began in Kuala Lumpur and the surrounding areas of the state of Selangor, with minor disturbances in Malacca. The government swiftly imposed a nationwide state of emergency and a curfew on May 16 in an effort to prevent further bloodshed.

All schools were closed indefinitely. Hye Keat Estate where we lived was a Chinese community and there was concern that, since it sat in a dead-end valley with only two exits of bridges across a river both on the south side, the Malays could easily attack and torch the only escape routes. Young men armed with machetes and sticks quickly formed a vigilante corps, taking turns through the night guarding the entrances against would-be attackers. Ah Wee joined them. Many nights I heard running footsteps and shouting, wondering if there were an actual attack on the estate.

Soon the Iban soldiers came and disbanded the vigilante corps. A curfew was imposed. Only essential personnel such as doctors and nurses were allowed to be out but under the escort of the soldiers or police. We felt besieged. After six o'clock we had to close our windows and doors, dim our lights, and stay indoors. With no TV or radio, we only heard rumors of violence: the Malays hacking a couple to death while they rode a motorbike by a Malay *kampong*; the Malays were attacked while in the cinema halls in the Chinese area. When such rumors circulated, the other ethnic group called for revenge and so the terror continued.

When the curfew was lifted in the morning, people emerged like moles to buy food and essential items. Soon the stores ran out of supplies. My father could not run his business, and Ah Yee could not feed us. The rice receptacle was long empty. She resorted to buying remnants of rice noodles used to feed chickens and ducks, and spending hours sorting through the short, broken pieces of rice sticks and separating them from dirt, hair, and pieces of wire. She washed them thoroughly, soaked them in water, and then fried them with some pickled vegetables, and when we were lucky, eggs. It was delicious. Since it was to be our only meal, we made the most of it. I could not recall ever having breakfast or lunch during those hard times. Consumed with the ravenous desire for the next meal, voracious, gnawing, insatiable hunger devoured and sapped my feeble energy. Ah Wee and my father were unaware of her plight, typically eating out or at work, and we did not complain.

The government came one day with a truckload of rice for distribution. Ah Yee was firm in her belief that if we accepted the handout, we had sunk to the level of beggars. Hunger drove people to swarm the lorry, scrambling to get their sack of rice. Yong, my younger sister, the practical one, went to fetch the bag of rice for us. Grateful to see the rice receptacle full again, we felt a little bit more secure, even if only for a few days.

I do not recall how long schools remained closed and when it was deemed safe for us to return. The curfew was in effect for at least eighteen months although the hours were shortened as time went on before it was eventually lifted. According to the police figures, about 200 people died, 150 people were wounded, and many ethnic Chinese women were raped during the race riots. Eyewitness accounts differed and placed the death toll between 700 and 1,000.

The May 13, 1969 riots were a significant event in that parliament was suspended and a temporary government body, the *Majlis Gerakan Negara* or the National Operations Council (NOC) took over. The first prime minister of the country, Tunku Abdul Rahman, resigned and Tun Abdul Razak succeeded him. The new government implemented a New Economic Policy reinforcing and broadening the scope of the affirmative policy started in 1965, favoring the Malays, including providing subsidies for their real estate purchases, quotas for public equity shares, and *Bumiputra* businesses with the aim to increase the Malay representation in both the private and public sectors. The NOC firmly believed that the root cause of the racial issues was the economic disadvantages suffered by the majority of Malays and in order to correct that, the economic and educational standards of the rural Malays needed to be raised. The policy that favored the Malays was one of the reasons I had to seek a scholarship from a foreign institution to further my education.

Malaysia is no exception when it comes to racial issues. I have not returned to live in my birth country to experience how the different races have lived and worked together since the race riots, but from what I have heard from my siblings, the ordinary people have learned to accept their cultural differences and live in relative harmony. I have lived in America for the greater part of my adult life; it too grapples with its own racial issues.

19

Rising in status but still not a Bumiputra

Form six was the pre-university program in Malaysia, based on the United Kingdom educational system. It was divided into lower and upper six and spanned two years. The science stream was subdivided into two groups, math and science. Lan Fong joined the math group, but I stayed with the science group. At this point, I became the first person in my family to go to form six in preparation for university.

It was 1969. St. George's opened its door to form five graduates from the Penang Chinese Girls' School to its form six classes. Almost all of them joined the math group for they were formidable. Just as Lan Fong and I were shunned by the original St. George's girls when we first arrived, the Chinese school students were ignored and looked down upon by the old St. George's girls, who prided themselves on their fluency in the Queen's English. The Chinese school students were more comfortable conversing in Mandarin, and this made it even more difficult for them to integrate.

Lan Fong and I went to a Chinese primary school so we were able to communicate freely with them in Mandarin. Sue spoke Mandarin at home, and so she became their spokesperson by default as she was then one of the two prefects in our class, besides Liling.

That year I was nominated to be on the Prefects Board. My having clinched first place in my class in form five helped. When we reached form six, we discarded our old uniforms and donned a white skirt and shirt with a pink, silver-gray, and white striped tie. Ah Yee had to dig into her pocket for the new uniform.

A week after the interview, the Prefects Board elected me to join their ranks, which required yet another uniform—a red skirt topped by a white shirt and a red tie with an embroidered crest. Then the whole tableau was finished off with a white blazer closed with a single large red button. Ah Yee sewed the skirt. I could still wear my white shirt. But the blazer had to be professionally tailored.

It so happened one of the prefects was selling her old blazer. Like many of the well-to-do families, she would be going to Australia for higher education. I met up with her in the library, and she handed me a bag containing her blazer. I brought it home and tried it on. It fit well. It took me by surprise when Ah Yee, against her frugal nature, decided I should go downtown to get a new one made by a tailor. I returned the blazer to the owner. A day or two later she confronted me with a group of her friends, telling me I had ruined her blazer, pointing at a patch of red hue on the white blazer around the red button. It was as though someone tried to wash it and the dye from the red button ran into the white part of the blazer. She threatened to report me to the headmistress if I refused to buy it, leaving me with no choice but to forgo getting a new blazer.

All the school clubs were vying for new members at the beginning of the new academic year and new teams of officers were to be elected by the members. There was quite a buzz in the class all day long, especially among the clique of clever girls, confident that their leader Liling would be elected the president of the Science Club since she was the secretary the year before. The Chinese girls harbored an intense dislike for this group, strategizing among themselves together with Sue how best to upset the election. They rallied all the Chinese girls to attend the Science Club meeting.

After school was over, we all trooped into the science building for the first meeting. The first order of business was the election of officers. Liling presided over the meeting as the past president already graduated and it was logical for a secretary to preside and to be the scribe at the blackboard. Her girls nominated her right away; she ran a hand over her flushed cheeks and pretended to turn away in shyness. Then there was a long pause. The girls from the Chinese school whispered from the back of the room.

When Liling was about to close the nomination, one of the Chinese girls raised her hand. Dropping a bombshell, she nominated me, seconded by most of the Chinese girls. The group of clever girls sitting in front turned around and stared at them. As there were no more nominations, Chui See, the former treasurer, took over from Liling.

Liling walked out of the room first and I followed, still not believing I had been nominated to run for the president of the Science Club. She turned around and glared at me, her arms crossed over her chest. We did not speak. She walked away from me to the farthest corner of the veranda. With both hands resting on the short wall, she sighed and stared out into the distance. We waited.

The election was conducted by a show of hands. When we were called in, Liling led the way. Applause broke out. Certain that it was for her, she waved and took the chalk from Chui See without looking at the tally of the number of votes for each candidate on the blackboard. I headed for my seat at the back, never thinking I would be elected. The applause kept up. The Chinese school girls swarmed around me and offered their congratulations.

Liling stole a look at the final tally; her face fell. Immediately she dropped the piece of chalk on the shelf and walked off the platform. Shocked, it took me a while to regain my composure. Then I realized, being the new president, I had to take over the election of the rest of the officers. Because Liling received fewer votes, she became vice president. As though it was not enough I had toppled her off her pedestal as the number one girl last year, now I was also the president of one of the most reputable clubs at St. George's.

Physical education was a large part of our curriculum. There were four sports houses that met separately for the first four days of the week. Because the temperature cooled off in the latter part of the afternoon, each sports house held its physical activities around four in the afternoon. What I lacked in skills in sports, I made up for with sheer determination and enthusiasm.

Like the clubs, the sports houses held their election for new officers on the first day of the house meeting. Again, out of the blue I was overwhelmingly elected to be the captain of Bass House and field hockey. It did not matter whether I was one of the most petite members of Bass House and had not won any championships in sports. Chui See, a Bass House member quickly spread the news of the election to Liling. In only a year I had risen to become a prefect, president of the Science Club, captain of Bass House and field hockey, assistant secretary of the Maths Society, business manager of the St. George's Girls' School Editorial Board, and a representative of the Sixth Form UNESCO Club.

We had sports meets twice a year. Mr. Lee, our sports teacher, asked me to run in the 400-meter race. He had seen me run and thought I had the endurance. Akbal Kaur, my Punjabi classmate, was recruited by her sports house to run the same race. She, like me, had not been training for track; the other two girls from the other houses were seasoned track runners. So, it would be a competition between Akbal and me to fight for third place.

When the gun went off, the two trained athletes took off. Akbal was much taller than me and she thought her long legs would help her to beat me. As we passed the 300-meter mark, the two girls were at least 30 meters ahead of us. Akbal and I were neck and neck; I could hear her grunting and muttering beneath her breath. For the last 20 meters, I sprinted, determined not to be the last, and beat her to the finish line.

Mr. Chan did not teach form six. Our new English teacher, Miss Teh, a Malayan University graduate, never missed an opportunity to blow her trumpet. Her buck teeth stood in the way of her enunciating her words clearly. She wore oversized blouses and long skirts. From day one, she looked down on the girls transferred from the Chinese school and made it a mission to make their lives miserable. She assigned us to write a short description of the telephone. That proved to be difficult, for few of us owned one and most had not even used or seen one. Instead of helping us to improve our writing, she mocked our clumsy attempt. Picking on the Chinese girls she read their essays aloud and threw their exercise books on the floor. "You call yourself a sixth-form student, you're worse than a primary school pupil. Shame on you!"

I missed Mr. Chan.

—

In 1963, Malaysia, a federation incorporating Malaya, Singapore, Sabah, and Sarawak, was formed. In the new federation, the urban Chinese were perceived to hold the majority of the wealth and controlled the Malaysian economy while the rural Malays were seen as poor. This disparity led to the 1964 race riot in Singapore where curfews were imposed. The Iban soldiers, considered a neutral party, were sent to various parts of Malaysia to keep the peace. Formerly known by the British as the Sea Dayaks, renowned for practicing head-hunting for tribal and territorial expansion, they were a strong and successful warring tribe. The Iban soldiers were also sent to keep the peace after the 1969 race riots.

While we were in secondary school, the Malaysian government implemented a five-year plan to include concrete steps to bring the Malays out of the villages into the cities for educational opportunities in order to boost their economic standing in society. *Bumiputras*, a term originating from the Sanskrit meaning son of the land, refers to Malays who practice Islam and speak Malay as their native tongue, and it also includes the indigenous people, the *Orang Asli* of Peninsular Malaya. Certain pro-*Bumiputra* policies were implemented as affirmative actions for them including generous quotas favoring them by lowering the standard for admission into government educational institutions, qualification for public scholarships, positions in government, and ownership in businesses. The government gave a stipend for the two *Bumiputras* in my class to attend secondary school whereas the rest of us from other ethnic groups had to pay a school fee. They received free textbooks while Kuan May and I had to scour the second-hand bookstores for ours.

So, it was not a surprise when one day the class erupted into a heated debate about the unfairness of the policies. Being overwhelmingly non-*Bumiputra*, the class wanted an equal chance at getting a scholarship and not being penalized for being ethnically Chinese or Indian. The economic power of Malaysia was in the hands of a small portion of the minority Chinese, many ordinary Chinese and Indians were from poor or middle-class families and they too needed an equal opportunity policy to help them along. The class *en masse* turned on Rosana and Aisha, the only Malays who benefited from the policies. Aisha, incidentally, was ethnically Chinese but had been adopted by a Malay family and was deemed a *Bumiputra*. She buried her head in her book, red in the face, leaving poor Rosana to try her level best to defend her position.

Our science teachers were the same teachers from form five, but our math teacher was Mrs. Wong, the form five substitute teacher for Mrs. Lin, our calculus teacher. Mrs.

Wong wore a loose unflattering dull-colored housecoat, looking perpetually pregnant, rumpled, and untidy, as though she had just rolled out of bed. Her short-cropped straight black hair framed a round, plain, bespectacled face. She read verbatim from the Math Mechanics book in a monotone that put us to sleep. Sue was not good at math and thought that by sitting next to me, my skill would rub off on her. I let her in on the secret that I too had a hard time following Mrs. Wong's teaching. Indeed, I had to teach myself at home by doing the problems on my own.

Problem: *A passenger train traveling at a steady speed of 60 mph leaves Kuala Lumpur at 12 noon for Province Wellesley, exactly 240 miles away. At the same instant, a freight train traveling at 50 mph leaves Province Wellesley for Kuala Lumpur. At the same high noon, a fly starts from the nose of the passenger train flies straight down the track towards the freight train. When the fly reaches the freight train it immediately turns around without pausing and heads toward the other train. It continues to do this until the two trains collide. If the fly travels at a steady speed of 80 mph, how many miles does the fly travel before the collision?*

I asked myself in the hot and sleepy classroom at high noon, did I really care?

20

Against all odds

In lower six my mind worked overtime, mulling over my future. I had no illusion that my father would be able to send me abroad despite his constant empty boastings to his friends. They congratulated him on his good fortune of having a smart daughter. While I did not tell my father about my awards, he had heard about them through Ah Wee. He was aware of our attending secondary school but was not in a position to stop us, since Ah Wee helped the family financially. I was first in my class for all the years I was in secondary school, winning prizes in most of the subjects. My bookworm nature had paid off. The Malaysian government offered a limited number of university scholarships to which everyone in the lower six class in the entire country applied. A big portion of them were designated for the *Bumiputras*. This made the jockeying for the few remaining precious scholarships even more competitive. I needed a backup plan if I hoped to continue with my education. In a year's time, I would be out of secondary school.

Some of my classmates left for England to attend nursing schools, receiving a stipend from the British government in return for a few years of service after completion. I was never in love with nursing and, besides, their parents had to foot the cost of their trip to England which my parents could never afford.

In form three, we could put down three career choices on a "career card." This card reappeared at the beginning of every academic year when we reconsidered our options and changed our choices. My first choice was to be an engineer. There were few woman engineers then, and I thought it would be great to be one of the first, never mind that I had no notion what being an engineer involved. Then I was at a loss what to put down as my second and third choices. The only people I had been exposed to in my short life were nurses and teachers, so I wrote down nurse and teacher.

Sometime during form four, Kuan May introduced me to a book she borrowed from the United States Information Service or USIS library: *The Night They Burned the Mountains* by Tom Dooley. It recounted his humanitarian efforts in Laos among the poor Hmong people during the troubled time of communism. Lan Fong told me about Dr. Albert Schweitzer and his medical missionary works in Gabon, Africa. I was very moved by Dr. Dooley's selfless service at great danger to himself. I was sufficiently inspired by both people, tucking them safely in the deep recesses of my mind.

The next time the career card was distributed, I changed my first choice to doctor. I was never keen on my second and third choices of being a nurse and a teacher. After secondary school, graduating students in Malaysia could apply to go to nursing schools or the Malayan Teachers College, the government paid them a stipend for such endeavors. Fong and Boon opted for nursing. Even if they aspired to go to university, there was no way they could attend without substantial financial aid. Coming right after independence, the young country needed all the teachers and nurses it could train. Our school did not have a counselor and we received no guidance; the career cards were filed away and I was not sure whether anyone ever took a look at them.

I was first introduced to the USIS at the Penang Pier when Mr. Khoo took our form one class on a field trip. We toured the library, watched a movie, and at the end, we were all given a library card which allowed us to borrow two books at a time for free, it was a ticket that opened the world to me. USIS was the first genuinely free library in Malaya and it served the whole of northern Malaya.

In 1817, the British set up the Penang Library, the oldest library in Malaya. It was founded to provide recreational reading for the European community and catered to the wealthy and prosperous as it required a high subscription and an entrance fee. In the nineteenth century, the membership of this exclusive library was a veritable Who's Who of society. It was located, during my time, in the supreme court building on Farquhar Street, less than a mile from the USIS, and it was not free. I visited it and was both in awe and intimidated by its elegant Corinthian columns supporting the high white ceilings with ornate chandeliers. I was never completely at ease there and felt like an intruder and an imposter. Although I could sit in the reading room of the library and read the books, I was not allowed to take them out.

In 1952, when the US established the USIS in the Indian House, an art deco building on Beach Street near Weld Quay, the director of the British Council Colonies' Department, Charles Wilmot, wrote to the representative of the British Council of Singapore that there should be a British Council's response to the American presence on Penang Island such as a British Council cultural center but he was not sure where he was to derive the funding. There began a barrage of complaints to Wilmot from other council representatives including R.M. Fry in 1951, "It will be noticed the USIS is beating us on the equipment and information side as they are bound to do in view of the funds at their disposal. The result of the council being insufficiently equipped in this way tends to make the Asiatic and the unthinking and narrow-minded European look down on us." But never mind whether the British lost face in this competition, the mere fact that there was no fee charged to me by the American establishment trumped the local exclusive Penang Library. The USIS provided the information sought by a poor student who could not afford a library membership to the Penang Library which made its exclusivity plainly felt as soon as one entered its portico.

Books were scarce in my family. I read my brother's Oxford English readers and learned about how people in England spent their holidays. In primary school, I saved up money to buy a few books of fairy tales for a bookcase that Kuan May and I built; we read them over and over. In standard four, there was a cupboard of books at the back of the classroom; we could peruse them but not take them home. The school had a big library and similar rules applied.

By the time I went to secondary school, there was still

no library from which to borrow books. Mr. Khoo did me a great service, and the USIS became a favorite haunt of mine, especially during the holidays when I had no place to go; there was no such thing as a family vacation or a day at the beach for a poor family such as mine. Still, I had to save up enough bus fare to spend a glorious day at the library. It started early in the morning. I spent many hours browsing through magazines and books and enjoyed a movie in the theater later in the day. My lunch was the cold drinking water from the fountain outside the bathroom, and I stayed till closing time with my stomach growling. To save a few *sen* off the bus fare I walked from the pier to the center of Georgetown to catch the bus home, nestling a couple of books in my arms. Ah Yee was not pleased I was away the whole day and not around to help her. She did not allow me to help with the cooking anyway, Kuan May had the honor of being her sous chef while all I got to do was cut up the vegetables and prepare the fish if she trusted me to do them well.

For one whole year, Kuan May and I competed with each other as to how many library books we could read. We kept a reading list and exchanged our library books with each other so we had more books to read before having to make the trek again. At the end of the year, Kuan May beat me on the number of books read.

It was in the USIS Library where I learned about my favorite American president, Abraham Lincoln. Next to the librarian's office was a reading nook for young readers. When I was tired of reading the magazines, I went there, sitting on the low chair, exploring the books on the bookshelves, and I found a number of books on Lincoln. Inspired by his difficult and poor childhood, his determination to educate himself reading by the light of the fireplace. As I read by the light of a kerosene lamp, I felt a kinship with him. He convinced me I could overcome any adversity; it was up to me to work hard.

On July 20, 1969, Apollo 11 landed on the moon. In the window showcase of the USIS were a model of the rocket ship and life-size cardboard pictures of the three astronauts who made the mission. I gazed at Neil Armstrong, my instant hero. My form five physics teacher, Mr. Chin, was understandably excited, imparting his knowledge of the gravitational force and the physics of orbiting and reentry into the atmosphere. At that time of my life, I was sure I wanted to do well in science, especially physics, and dared to dream of becoming an astronaut. It did not matter if I were not an American. That year for my science project, I built a model of the rocket that launched the astronauts to the moon.

Meng Kee's Chinese professor's brother returned from America for his summer break from an American university. He told Kuan May that American universities offered scholarships to foreign students and that I should look into it. During one of my math classes, I let my mind wander about my future. Increasingly I worried about what was to become of me if I did not get a university scholarship. I told Sue of my plan to visit the USIS after school to find out more about American colleges and universities. That caught her attention. She sat up straight and stared at the blackboard for a while. Then she leaned over to me and whispered, "I'm coming with you." Mrs. Wong caught her talking to me and said in a loud monotone, "Sue, please pay attention!"

After school Sue sent her chauffeur home and we took the bus to the pier. At the USIS, my heart sank to see that the librarian was a stern-looking woman outfitted in a *cheong sum* just like Ma Ooi. Her sleek black hair was combed back smoothly into a bouffant, her reading glasses hung from her neck. Her office was encased in a room with walls half made of glass so we could see her clearly. She returned my gaze over the rim of her glasses. I timidly told her our wish to apply to American colleges and universities and asked her to direct us to any reference books.

There was a long pause and a steely stare as she sized us up to see if we were worthy of her attention. I fidgeted. She stood up, walked from her desk across the room to the row of bookshelves behind us, and with her long fingers dug out two volumes, each was at least three inches thick: *The Complete Book of Colleges: The Mega-Guide to over 1,000 Colleges and Universities* listed by state in alphabetical order.

We followed her out of her office to the children's reading room. She plunked down the heavy volumes on the round table. Sue and I settled down with our notebooks and each took a volume and perused through the fine print. We agreed to start from either end of the books, she from the state of Alabama and I from the state of Wyoming, and meet in the middle. After spending some time flipping through the books, we decided there was too much information and our method of searching for suitable colleges to apply to was too tedious; it would take us forever to find what we wanted. We had to set some criteria.

We carefully avoided the big universities and concentrated on small colleges, afraid we would be lost otherwise.

We looked for colleges that offered scholarships to foreign students. During my secondary school years, I elected to study the geography of the US over Europe. I learned that the northeast had many colleges and universities, in particular, my textbook singled Boston out as a hub of education. I told Sue I would concentrate my search in the northeast, especially Massachusetts. The lyrics of the song "Massachusetts" by the Bee Gees played steadily in my head.

We worked for several hours that afternoon. My piece of bread with jam that morning was long gone; I tried to suppress my growling stomach by wandering to the drinking fountain. Soon we learned about the Ivy League Schools and the Seven Sisters Colleges. The Ivy League Schools were predominantly male and almost all of them were universities. I was interested in smaller schools so I did not look further into them. Perhaps because of our persistence, the librarian brought us to her office and showed us specific college catalogs stashed in her bookshelves; catalogs from some of the Seven Sisters colleges—Mt. Holyoke, Radcliffe, Smith, but she had no catalog from Wellesley College. She informed us we had to sit for the SAT (Scholastic Aptitude Test) and TOEFL (Test of English as a Foreign Language) before our application for college admission. I worried about the money for the examinations.

We made several more visits to the USIS. Sue branched out to the heartland of America, but I wished to be near the oceans. She worried about racial discrimination, falling in love with a Caucasian, having mixed-race children, societal acceptance of them, and most of all about her mother, for by now her father had passed away. These were not my immediate concerns. first I had to get accepted to a college which would also offer me a full scholarship.

One Saturday while we were in the reference library researching, a group of white-uniformed boys trooped into the librarian's office. They were students from Chung Ling Chinese Boys' School, a top-notch Chinese secondary school on the island. One of their alumni had just returned from Princeton University for his summer vacation; he was giving a talk about university life in America and how to apply for schools there. The librarian asked him whether we could join them. For our sake, he gave his talk in English but peppered it with Mandarin. He met with the boys individually and interviewed them for Princeton. The librarian asked him to do us a favor by looking at our lists of schools, transcripts, and advising us as to which schools we should apply.

Sue and I met with the Princeton man separately. Rubbing his chin, he spent some time looking over my transcripts and list. When he crossed out Wellesley I was disappointed as I had learned from the librarian that Wellesley was an elite school, but I did not ask him his reason for eliminating it. When Sue emerged from her meeting, Wellesley remained on her list.

I wrote to the various schools for application forms and catalogs. I borrowed money from Ah Yee to buy aerograms, the cheapest way to send a letter overseas. On the square blue piece of paper, I cramped in as many facts as possible about my background and why I wanted to go to school in America, making grids on the aerogram to display my secondary school marks. Finally, and most importantly, I also asked to have my application fee waived. I could not afford it.

One afternoon after school, our whole lower six class trooped down to the education department to file our application for a scholarship to the University of Malaya, the only university in the country at that time. I remembered climbing the stairs a couple of years before to state my case for a transfer to St. George's. I looked around at the swarm of schoolgirls excitingly filling out the form, a fraction of the students from the whole country vying for a few miserable scholarships. My chances of getting one of these scholarships were very slim. As we trooped downstairs after handing in our applications, I was determined more than ever to get into an American college.

Within a few weeks, the postman delivered thick envelopes stuffed with application forms and catalogs. I waded through them, eliminating the schools that had refused to waive the hefty application fees. I made photocopies of my transcripts at the pier, all the while borrowing money from Ah Yee, promising somehow to pay her back. For my college essay, I wrote about my life growing up on this tiny island in the Indian Ocean and my dream of getting a higher education to end the cycle of poverty forever plaguing my family.

One evening at the Reservoir Gardens Baptist Church, which Sue had started attending with me since she lived in the area, she excitedly showed me a postcard from Wellesley College. It was a picture of the Galen Stone Tower of Green Hall standing tall over the rest of the collegiate Gothic architecture of the academic quads of Founders Hall and the gently sloping green field in the foreground; it resembled a picture taken right out of the English countryside. If my parents had the means, England would have been the place where I would like to go to school. I stared at it for a long time and fell in love with it.

At the end of the service, we sat on the church steps, still looking at the postcard. I asked, "Do you mind if I apply to Wellesley?" There was a long silence.

"My marks are not as good as yours. I will not stand a chance of getting admitted if you apply." Looking pensively into the distance at the shimmering lights of Georgetown, she finally turned to me. "Go ahead."

I wrote to Wellesley and a few weeks later the same pastoral postcard arrived in the mail. I wondered why the man from Princeton crossed out Wellesley from my list of schools.

Along with the application came the request for letters of recommendation, one of which was to be from an English teacher certifying my proficiency in the English language. It seemed proper to ask my current form six teacher, Miss Teh.

Smith and Radcliffe College urged me to complete upper six and sit for my A-Levels before applying which would mean staying till the end of the academic year in Malaysia and delaying college by another year. This was not an option for me. I feared my father would complain about me eating *see png* while living at home for a year; it would be agonizing. Among my applications, I included two schools to which recent St. George's girls had been admitted: Mills College in California and Marygrove College in Michigan.

One bright Saturday morning, Sue and I sat for our SATs in the auditorium of the USIS. We were the only girls, the rest were the boys from Chung Ling Chinese Boys' School. I had no Kaplan or Princeton review classes as most American children did to help them achieve a high score. I had never heard of them and could never afford them anyway. All summer long, the boys were coached by the Princeton man. The Malaysian education was based on the British system which required written essays; the SATs on the other hand relied on multiple choice questions, a completely foreign concept. I only had the sample test questions on the application form for the SAT test to look at. I went to take our test cold, with no preparation whatsoever.

One of the colleges notified me that they were still waiting for Miss Teh's letter. Fortuitously she came to the Reservoir Gardens Baptist Church as a visitor and I told her about her missing letter. Giving me a smirk, she told me she had not sent the letter because I did not provide her with a stamped addressed envelope. I was crushed. All this time I thought my applications were complete. We had English class three times a week, she had never once mentioned her need for a stamped addressed envelope; she must have been aware that my future depended on my application.

I asked Mr. Chan, my form five English teacher, to write me a letter instead. It was difficult for me to ask any teacher for a recommendation letter because I was shy to reveal my secret aspirations. But Mr. Chan, after listening to me, cleared his throat and wished me good luck. He did not ask for a stamped addressed envelope.

Wellesley requested I fill out a financial aid form accounting for my parents' income, investments, and real estate. They had none. I reported Ah Wee's income which, when converted to US dollars, was dismal.

By November I completed our lower six. In mid-December, I was selected to attend *Khemah Muhibbah* or Goodwill Camp for a week in the Uplands School, the International School of Penang on Penang Hill, along with many students from all over the country to promote national unity (*untok bersatu dan perpaduan kebangsaan*).

Attending *Khemah Muhibbah* was the longest time I was away from home. I was not homesick. I slept in a bunk bed in the dormitories with our camp counselor, Miss Florence Scully. The food was culturally appropriate, no pork or beef in deference to the Muslims and the Hindus. I could not get used to eating mutton, which smelled like a farm. The most enjoyable time was singing around the evening bonfire. *Khemah Muhibbah* brought to bear that Malaysia was a truly multi-racial country.

Then came the annual dance for all the prefects from the secondary schools on Penang Island. I attended it, vaguely telling my parents that it was just a meeting. They did not query me further, even as the "meeting" took place in the evening. I did not get home until after ten at night, a rather late hour at that time of my life. During the dance in the big hall at the Penang Free School, we did group dancing and never attempted to dance as couples, avoiding at all cost any kind of close body contact. I remembered taking the green Lim Seng Seng bus home, tiptoeing into the dark hallway, making as little noise as possible for fear of waking up my father. Only the tick-ticking of my neighbor, Ah Fatt, doing his end-of-day accounting on his abacus, could be heard. After brushing my teeth and changing into my pajamas, I slipped under the covers next to Kuan May. She had long stopped telling me bedtime stories. Although we remained close in my secondary school days, I had begun to spread my wings and no longer followed her lead.

In January I continued into upper six. Sue and I kept our fingers crossed for our college acceptance results which would come in March. Schools in Malaysia started in January and ended in December. Not knowing whether we would get accepted to start school in the US in the fall, we continued to prepare for our A-Levels which would take place at the end of the year.

By March after school, I waited anxiously for the young Indian postman delivering mail on a red postman bicycle still emblazoned with the crest of Windsor, a remnant from the old British colonial days. He arrived around two in the afternoon, at the peak of the heat, and rang his bell. I had learned that a thin letter meant rejection and good news came in the form of a fat thick envelope.

Marygrove College accepted me with a partial scholarship. Mills College accepted me with no financial aid; this was equivalent to not being accepted. I was crestfallen.

Then March 2, 1970 came. I remember that afternoon well. It was as sweltering as every other afternoon. The postman handed me a single, thin envelope. I took it without much hope of any good news. Taking a deep breath, I left my finger under the flap and waited a moment. I hadn't even looked at the return address, so I didn't know which school it was.

The distinct font of Wellesley College at the top of the page caught my eye.

It is with genuine pleasure that we write to inform you that the Board of Foreign Student Admission has voted to accept your application for admission to Wellesley College for September 1970. Full scholarship assistance of $3,440 has been awarded to you, also.

That academic year, Wellesley accepted three girls from the Island of Penang alone. Besides me, Wei Ni our former form five class monitor who went to Australia for higher studies, and Kah Peng who turned out to be the childhood sweetheart of the man from Princeton! Now I knew why Wellesley had been scratched from my list and not Sue's. I was a competitor for his girlfriend.

I told Kuan May the good news. After all, it was she who planted the idea in my head to look into America to further my education. Unbeknownst to my form one teacher, Mr. Khoo, who introduced me to the USIS one hot sultry afternoon, he and the USIS forever changed my life. The Americans beat the British in the pursuit of my education all because of the free library.

That evening when my mother sat on the bench on the front porch enjoying the breeze after a day of chores, I showed her my acceptance letter and told her I would soon leave for America to go to school. I was not sure she understood. She had already lost a daughter to America, a daughter whom she had not seen in years. She did not say much in reply, but I was happy beyond words.

Sue was accepted into Doane College in Nebraska. She worried about not meeting any Asian men in the heartland of America. I was more concerned about finding the money to get a passport, a student visa, and a one-way ticket to America.

The Kent State shooting in 1970 splashed on the front page of *The Straits Times*. Boon subscribed to *Life* magazine and brought home stories of the shooting. I was horrified at the picture of the young lady crying for help over the limp body of a co-ed lying face down on the campus ground, picturing myself dodging bullets on the campus of Wellesley or holing up in the dormitory while there was widespread chaos in the US. How was I going to be safe?

By now everybody at home knew about my going to America. Ah Wee said, *"Mai Kee lah."* Don't go. We forgot that America was vast and imagined the violence was commonplace in all college campuses, including Wellesley College; it was hard for him to believe there were peaceful campuses in the States.

Miss Cheah, our biology teacher suddenly became maternal and protective. She sat in her biology laboratory on a stool across from Sue, Wei Ni, and me, telling us that going overseas carried with it many temptations and we had to be careful. I looked at Wei Ni, who had spent over a year in Melbourne and returned unscathed. Miss Cheah wanted us to reconsider given the unrest in the college campuses in America. I had already made up my mind that nothing, including the shootings on the campuses, was going to hold me back from this opportunity. There was nothing here that offered me anything like this wonderful scholarship. We listened politely and did not argue with her.

I wrote to Fong and her husband in Spokane, Washington, and they bought me a one-way ticket on Pan Am stopping overnight at the Ambassador Hotel in Hong Kong, and then on to San Francisco. It cost them $500. They sent me $200 for expenses, and my preparation to go abroad began. Kuan May took me right outside the passport office under the shades of the flame of the forest trees where there were scribes who, for a fee, typed up my application for a passport. I went to the Penang Adventist Hospital to get a required medical examination from an American doctor. For a number of years now I had a slowly expanding, unsightly painful growth on the top of my left hand. I consulted a Sikh surgeon at the Penang General Hospital; he told me I could either keep it or have it removed surgically and live with a scar. The American doctor at the Adventist hospital told me I could smash it with a Bible.

"Are you trying to smuggle something into the US?" he said as he tucked my hand into his belly and applied steady pressure on it. I felt a sharp pain, and the thing popped. Beneath my skin was the gelatinous content of the burst ganglion cyst.

I bought a carry-on and a suitcase. Kuan May had a handyman add four little wheels at the base of the navy-blue suitcase and a pull strap. I carefully painted my name "Miss Lai Kwan Kew" in white paint near the handle. There were hardly any warm clothes to choose from in the stores so Kuan May had Pek See, her seamstress friend, make me three dresses of thin material, a short-sleeve frilly blouse, three floral print miniskirts, and a checkered pattern suit. I bought a pair of blue jeans, two pairs of sneakers, and one pair of plaid dress shoes. I did not know at the time that I was completely unprepared for the cold frigid winter of New England. As a farewell present, I bought a bottle of body lotion for Ah Yee to soothe her dry scaly skin. I did not have the money to pay her back the cost of my college applications, and she did not ask.

I was left with a $20 bill for my trip halfway around the world to America. Growing up I heard stories of Chinese immigrants coming to Malaya with a few coins in their pocket in the eighteenth and nineteenth centuries and years later through hard work, making themselves a fortune. I wondered whether I would be like one of them, a girl striking out to *Mei Guo*, America, which means beautiful country in Mandarin, with twenty dollars in her pocket, hoping to change her fate.

Sue and I applied for student visas. We had to wait for the US embassy in Kuala Lumpur to notify us for an interview. All my life, I left the island only twice, taking the ferry from Penang to Prai in Province Wellesley to visit Boon, and Ipoh on the peninsula to visit Meng Kee. The US embassy called Sue for an interview and her brother drove her there. I went with her on the off-chance the embassy would see me. I could not afford the train fare to Kuala Lumpur if I were to make the trip on my own. I did not worry about the mechanics questions that were frequently posed by Mrs. Wong, my math teacher: *Two buses left Prai at the same time moving in opposite directions. One traveled at a rate of 5 miles per hour faster than the other traveling at 30 mph. After 3 hours they were 375 miles apart. How far did each bus travel?*

I did not care how far each bus traveled, all I cared was that I was closing in on a visa to America.

We stayed overnight in Sue's brother's messy apartment. The next day he dropped us off at the US embassy. We waited. Sue was called in, and I asked whether I could be seen. To my relief, they agreed to see me. I had the letter of acceptance and financial aid from Wellesley. The person who interviewed me told me I had been accepted by a renowned school. We received our student visas the same day.

I was to start a new chapter of my life. I did not share with anyone that I was not planning to come back to Malaysia. The recent race riots were fearsome and reflected the simmering racial tension of the time, a rude awakening for second-class citizens like me.

The government responded to the 1969 race riots with a "New Economic Policy" (NEP) aimed at improving the lot of the *Bumiputras* with preferences in university admissions and for civil-service jobs. Billed in 1971 as a temporary measure, the NEP has become central to a system of corrupt patronage; the government continues with a quota plan which seemed lopsided in helping the *Bumiputras*. Malaysia's Chinese and Indian citizens are relegated to second-class citizens despite their years of contributions to the building of the country.

Most universities in Malaysia reserved seventy percent or more of their places for *Bumiputras*. Chinese and Indian students whose parents could afford to send them flocked instead to private and foreign institutions. Those who left often did not return home. A World Bank study in 2011 found that about one million Malaysians left the country, which had a total population of twenty-nine million. Most were highly educated Chinese. Some sixty percent of the emigrants cited "social injustice" as an important reason for leaving Malaysia. Critics argued that the economic and educational policies favoring the *Bumiputras* contributed to a brain drain, racial polarization, and a feeling of marginalization among the non-Malays. A survey in 2008 found that seventy-one percent of Malaysians agreed that race-based affirmative action was obsolete and should be replaced with a merit-based policy.

My father and Ah Wee talked about moving again. By the time my family was ready to move, I would have left for the United States. The government broke ground next to the small complex of terraced housing at Boundary Road by our old orchard home, to build several high-rise, low-cost flats—affordable housing for the urban poor. The project started when we were still living in Rifle Range where the remains of the victims of the Imperial Japanese Army's Sook Ching massacres were discovered; it was one of many mass graves on the island.

A German construction company spearheaded the housing project. The newspaper was filled with news of the construction of several seventeen- to eighteen-story high-rises of prefabricated concrete blocks. Each unit would have a single bedroom. We were then living in a rented house with three bedrooms. I had trouble picturing my parents and the remainder of my siblings being crowded into one small bedroom. What were the government or the German developers thinking? Didn't they know that the low-income families in Penang bred many children? Ah Wee could apply for a unit for himself and my father for a second, these would ease the congestion. They would pay a mortgage to the Penang Development Corporation and eventually own the units, a far better fate than paying rent to our landlady with nothing to show for it at the end.

I had few possessions to speak of. I packed the new shoes and clothes, my chemistry and math books, a few of my notebooks, and a pack of my class pictures and those of my siblings. That pretty much took up most of the space in my bags. With considerable pain, I burned most of my things that I could not pack, including the diary I kept in my teens—stories with illustrations, copies of my favorite poems—in a bonfire in the rubbish heap across the street from our rented home. I watched my past being erased as the pages of the diary curled and browned with the heat and then burst into flames. I left my favorite books, *Alice in Wonderland* and *Through the Looking Glass* in the Formica cabinet, hoping to retrieve them one day when I returned to visit.

One evening before I left for America, I sat on the bench next to Ah Yee on the front porch. I reached over and hugged her. She immediately stiffened and shrank ever so slightly from such close physical contact. Despite her small stature and quiet nature, she had been resourceful and a pillar of towering strength. She came through for us a thousand times over.

I thought about the time when I had resolutely informed her I would not get married, be lorded over by a man and beholden to him for all my needs and wants. Granted that had been during my pre-adolescent years. Had I hurt her feelings in any way considering the fact that fate doled her a challenging and difficult life in a society where women were considered less than men? I was determined to get myself an education, a career, and be financially independent even if I did get married. Wellesley College's offer of education would open many doors for me. I was sad to leave my mother, my family, my home, and my country, but I was happy to start a new chapter. It was fortuitous that a women's college offered a place to a young lady who had been told all her life that girls were useless. The time had come for me to show my father he was very wrong indeed.

21

Farewell to Penang

My bags were packed. I hummed "Leaving on a Jet Plane," Kuan May's favorite hit when she was dating an Iban soldier, Mike, who came to keep the peace after the race riots.

A romantic song about the parting of two lovers. It resonated with me. I was leaving my home country, a place where I grew up, filled with memories of happiness, sorrow, family, love, friendship, infinite struggles, courage, and resilience; a place where my character developed. Indeed, I truly did not know when I would be back.

Early in the morning, I waved goodbye to Ah Yee, standing on the front porch next to my three- and five-year-old sisters, innocent faces marked by small pouting mouths, faces I was not likely to see for a number of years. They would be grown if and when I came back to visit. I knew even then I would not be returning to live in Malaysia. This would be my true farewell to Penang.

Kuan May, Ah Wee, and my father came to the Penang International Airport. We stood around awkwardly, keeping our distance. Physical closeness and the showing of emotion was not part of my upbringing; I could not imagine shedding tears or throwing my arms around them.

Finally, Kuan May broke the silence and said, "Don't forget to write."

Ah Wee quickly chimed in in English, "Keep yourself out of trouble. There's no one there to help you."

My father shuffled about in his flip-flops, running his fingers through his thinning gray hair, "*Buay chou la.*" Time to go.

I had no idea what went through my father's mind seeing a second daughter off to America. Fong left five years earlier and had not returned. I was leaving for very different reasons, possibly of higher standing in his eyes. Most importantly I would no longer eat *see png.*

Through the airplane window, I could see them in the viewing gallery on the second floor, wondering when I would set my eyes on them again.

Many middle-aged foreign ladies boarded the plane. Many of them were from America.

The plane cruised along the runway. Soon Kuan May, Ah Wee, and my father became mere specks in the distance.

This was my first flight and my longest journey away from home. Strangely, I was not afraid but was at peace. The plane took off and went through the clouds. It took a sharp turn and banked its left wing downward, for a brief moment the island loomed into view and I said a silent farewell. I was to embark on an adventure of my own in a strange foreign land.

As I settled in my seat, many of the passengers around me were chattering away, and the woman sitting next to me asked me where I was going. I told her I was going to school in America.

"Where?" she asked.

"Wel-les-ley College," I answered.

"Oh," she turned to the other women on the plane and said excitedly, "She's going to Welles-ley." The oohs and aahs echoed through the plane.

I noticed she pronounced Wellesley as though it were a two-syllable word.

She turned to me and said, "Well, do you know Wellesley College is one of the most distinguished schools in America? You must be a very smart young lady."

I wished my father were there.

I had escaped the yoke of the traditional role a woman was expected to play—marriage and motherhood. Like the *burung layang-layang* I admired, I was free at last to pursue my own destiny.

I had taught myself to fly.

Afterword

My father passed away when he was eighty-five years old. Before that, he remained active, riding his bicycle and socializing with friends until he became ill one day. He implored his children not to bring him to the hospital; he was ready to die, feeling that his day had come. My siblings took him to the hospital against his wishes and he was diagnosed with leukemia. He stayed only a short time, requesting to be discharged, wishing to die at home.

The first telegram I received assured me that my father was doing well and I should not make plans to hurry home. My second child, Cara, was then four months old. The second telegram was more ominous. Shortly after that, at two in the morning, the dreaded phone call came. My sister Fong telephoned to break the news that he had passed away. I froze in my chair. Deep inside I felt I had lost a part of myself; there was an emptiness. She and I quickly made plans to fly home, me with my two young children. It would be my third trip home since I left, almost thirteen years before.

Back home, I learned that at his hospital bed, my father had repeatedly asked when Fong and I would be coming home, he wanted to see us one last time. We missed his funeral as that had to be quickly accomplished in the tropical heat. Fong and I paid our respects at the Christian cemetery. His resting place was in a quiet spot in a shady lot, befitting a busy man who fought all his life for a living. My father had converted to Christianity later in his life.

At the end of his long life, he had enjoyed a few grandchildren. He could be proud of the legacy he left behind, boys and girls alike. All his children were gainfully employed and the younger ones went for higher education. Boon emigrated to America, moving his whole family from a stable financial situation to start anew. Fong had her nursing degree from Malaysia, and Boon graduated as a hospital assistant. America did not recognize their degrees and they had to go back to school. Fong earned a graduate nursing degree. Boon decided to train to be a technologist in a cardiac catheterization unit, and he was so skillful that he could teach the fellows in training the techniques with his eyes closed; those were his own words. I am a medical doctor with a specialty in infectious diseases. I was my father's first child to obtain a graduate degree.

My mother was a young widow, and true to the prediction of her evil aunt, she was surrounded by her loving children, grandchildren, and great-grandchildren. Ah Wee and Lian Hua took care of her until Ah Wee died in 2020. Lian Hua continued caring for her until my mother passed away on June 2, 2022, just a week shy of her 96th birthday. In her old age, she suffered from dementia, slowly forgetting about us, lost in her own world where none of us could reach. The longer I was away from home, the more her memory of me retreated further and further into the abyss. I am the *burang layang-layang* that flew the coop a long time ago, and I have never looked back.

Fong, my feisty sister, fell in love with Pastor Charles Adams at the Peniel Church and moved to the US to marry him. Marrying a white man was taboo in my father's book. She returned home with her husband a few years later to make peace with my father. They parted on speaking terms. She passed away in her fifties from the complications of Lupus despite having received a kidney from me.

Wan, my sister who was adopted by my uncle and aunt, lives on the mainland and is married with three children. It took her a while to reconcile with my family. Apparently, her son persuaded her that it was important for her to forgive; her siblings had nothing to do with her being given away. She came to say goodbye to me at the airport when I came for a visit, though there was no time for me to catch up with her. I met her again at my mother's funeral service but only to find out our dialect barrier did not allow us to have a meaningful conversation. She had learned about her adoption in her teens.

Kuan May, my closest companion growing up, was two years older than me. She was always the instigator in our escapades. She planted the seed of the possibility of my continuing my education in an American college when she received a tip from a family member of Meng Kee's boss, the Chinese professor, that I could apply for a scholarship. The impetus to change my life and to escape the fate of my mother gave me the confidence and courage to strike out alone. In secondary school, although she and I remained close, I no longer followed her lead, veering onto a different path. After I was accepted into college, Kuan May guided me through my passport application and helped me to get ready for my trip, acting as my big sister, selflessly embracing my success as her own. She worked as a graphic technician at the Universiti Sains Malaysia which she once dreamed of attending. She is married and has two children and two grandchildren.

I did not return home until seven years later when I finally saved up enough money to pay for a roundtrip ticket, spending all my summers working for my expenses and saving for the trip, while many of my foreign student friends went back home almost every year to visit their families during their summer break. In the process I grew to become fiercely independent, earning my own upkeep. Although Malaya is my birthplace, my home now is in America, *Mei Guo,* the beautiful country, this is where I was given the chance to grow and determine how I should spend my life, and most of all, to live a life with a purpose to serve, to make a difference in the world and in a small way in someone's life.

Ironically, my father, who was so concerned about perpetuating the Lai family line, would now have to depend on his grandson, Nathaniel, Beng's son, to make it a reality. His grandson, Clement, Boon's son, has so far given him three beautiful granddaughters.

My husband, Scott, came back with me on my second trip home. On our way back from a family reunion on Penang Hill, while getting off the funicular train, my father, with a sweeping nonchalant gesture of his hand, announced to his friends working at the train station, "This is my daughter, home from America."

He finally acknowledged me as his *cha-bó-kiá.*

Author's Note

Many of the names have been changed to protect the privacy of the people mentioned in this book. This memoir is written from my perspective alone; it is as true as the vagaries of memory, time, and interpretation of events would allow. Any variations from the remembrances of those involved are to be expected and I beg patience, forgiveness, and forbearance in this regard.

I had already begun my memoir after leaving academia to focus on humanitarian work when my daughter, Cara, asked me to write about my early life so I would leave my children a legacy. It has been a labor of love, writing on and off for the past several years. In the interim I have had a wild ride in my varied humanitarian efforts spanning several continents, spending time in HIV/AIDS education and providing medical relief in natural disasters, outbreaks of diseases, refugee camps, and war-torn nations. I dreamed about doing such humanitarian work when I was young. I was able to do so because Wellesley College took a leap of faith and accepted me into their academic halls so many years ago to fulfill their mission of "providing an excellent liberal arts education to women who will make a difference in the world."

In many of my volunteering efforts in refugee camps, I have met many families—fathers, mothers, children of all ages—who fiercely cling to the belief that there is a better future awaiting them despite all odds. Few countries extend a helping hand to accept them as citizens; some host countries have strict rules excluding refugees from getting higher education. They remain in limbo, and their futures and those of their children hang in the balance.

For every child who escapes poverty and rises up to become a contributing member of society, there are many more who are left behind and do not make it. None has a choice where they are born or who their parents are. Despite their best efforts, they do not have the opportunities to determine their own destiny. They remain invisible to the world, mired in unspeakable hardship at every turn.

I was one of the lucky few.

Yes, I made it. Through fierce determination and hard work. But these would have counted for naught if I had not received help from Wellesley College and their faith that a young girl half a world away was worth investing in. When I arrived in the fall of 1970, many of the Seven Sisters Colleges were becoming co-ed under tremendous waves of social pressure. But my alma mater remains staunch in its empowerment of women's education and belief in its motto, *non ministrari sed ministrare*.

In 1957, Malaya gained its independence from the British. In 1963, Malaysia was established when Singapore and the colonies of Sabah and Sarawak in northern Borneo joined Peninsular Malaya. In 1965, Singapore seceded from the federation to become an independent republic. Malaysia has a complex multiracial population with diverse cultural backgrounds. There are three main ethnic groups: the Malays, the Chinese, and the Indians. The Malays, the predominant group, consist of about sixty-four percent of the population, the Chinese twenty-five percent, and the Indians, seven percent.

Bumiputra, a term originating from the Sanskrit meaning son of the earth, refers to Malays who practice Islam and speak Malay as their native tongue, and it also includes the indigenous people, the *Orang Asli* of Peninsular Malaya, and the tribal people of Sabah and Sarawak. Parliament started to use the term in 1965 and certain pro-*Bumiputra* policies were implemented as affirmative actions for them by lowering the standard for admission into government educational institutions and qualification for public scholarships, positions in government, ownership in businesses, and native reservations of land at the expense of the significant Chinese population. The intent was to raise the economic and educational standards of the rural Malays.

The special privileges were to expire in fifteen years unless parliament extended them. After the race riots of 1969, the policies under the rubric of the New Economic Policy (NEP)—a more aggressive form of the affirmative action policy for the *Bumiputras*—extended the old policies and adding subsidies for real estate purchases, quotas for public equity shares, and general subsidies to *Bumiputra* businesses. Initially intended to be a temporary measure, these race-based policies are still in effect today. Although the policies have succeeded in creating a significant urban Malay middle class, they have not eradicated poverty among the rural Malays. Many Malaysians feel these privileges should not continue indefinitely and that a merit-based policy not based on race should replace them, but others argue they should not have a sunset clause.

In 1969, when I applied for a Malaysian university scholarship, I could not see myself overcoming the affirmative actions in favor of one racial group. The external lifeline extended to me from Wellesley College, in the form of a full scholarship, was crucial.

So, for every child who is unlucky to be born into an impossibly difficult social situation, to overcome and rise above all that, they not only have to possess the necessary ingredients of sheer determination and persistence, there has to be a fundamentally good educational foundation, which existed on my island, and an offer of solid financial aid for further studies. Educating girls and women is key to ending the cycle of the sexist nature of poverty. It opens the door for them to make stronger life choices, including delaying marriage and unintended pregnancies. The pay-off for educating women comes through economically, socially, and politically.

Acknowledgements

Writing a memoir invariably involves people who grew up with me and impacted my becoming the person I am today. I am grateful to them for allowing me to include them in telling my story. My perspectives, interpretation, and memory of events may drastically differ from theirs, so I beg forbearance and forgiveness.

I started writing this coming-of-age story several years ago with the intent of leaving a legacy for my children so that they understood what life was like for their mother and her siblings, and that despite the hardship and poverty, one could hope to rise above all that and achieve an inconceivable dream.

For the last ten years, I have worked with refugees from various countries, in particular the Syrians, the Rohingya, and many from the sub-Saharan African nations, and seen first-hand the desperation of the refugees and their parents who wish for the best for their children. They not only have to struggle for their daily needs of food, shelter, and medical care, they have to get through reams of bureaucracy to get themselves out of their statelessness. Living in a refugee camp, without a country, safety, stability, and most of all, with no guarantee of an education, would mean a very bleak future for them and their children. I understand their predicament and am grateful for the fact that I grew up in a peaceful nation. They forever remind me that we as humans should never forget their plight and their thirst for a brighter future. They will always be in my thoughts and prayers for their courage and resilience in the face of extreme adversities.

I want to thank my mother, who recently passed away, for bringing us up through very difficult situations, and my brother, Boon, for reading parts of my memoir and bringing my remembrances of events into a sharper focus. I respected the wishes of some of my siblings for wishing to remain anonymous. Despite that, they are still truly part of the story and without them, this memoir could not have become a reality.

Finally, I would like to thank Amie McCracken for her astute guidance and a clear-eyed vision for the arc of my story.

Other Books by this Author

Lest We Forget: A Doctor's Experience
with Life and Death During the Ebola Outbreak

Into Africa, Out of Academia: A Doctor's Memoir

Vine Leaves Press

Enjoyed this book?
Go to *vineleavespress.com* to find more.
Subscribe to our newsletter: